The inhuman

or
war within Man

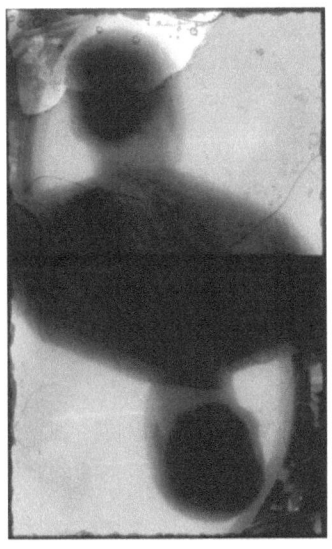

Bernard Gast

Translated from French by Raphaël Loison

I Gallery Editions

Collection Essays (Philosophy & Aesthetics)

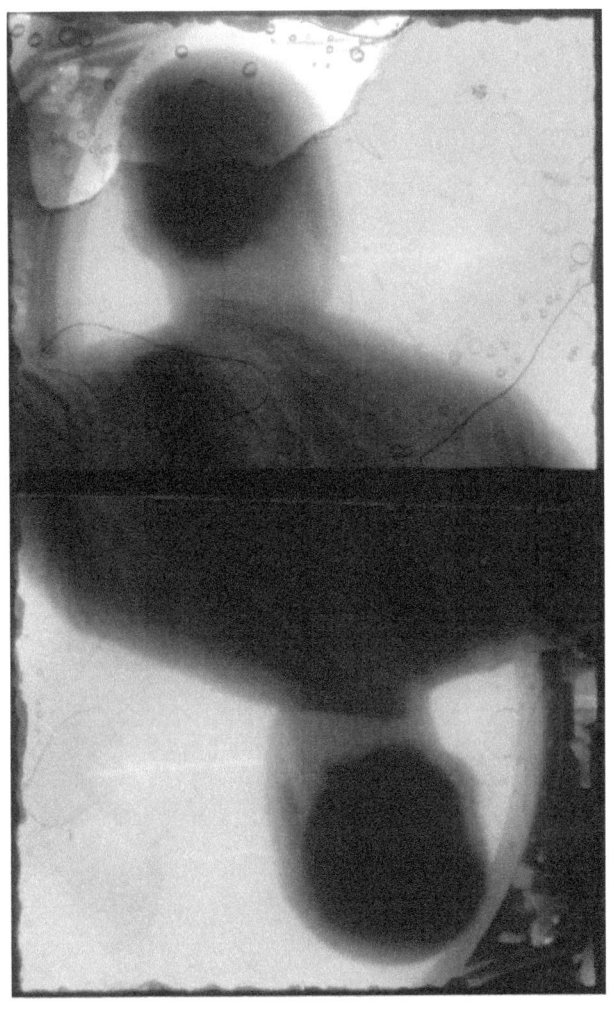

Copyright © 2022   I Gallery Editions

All rights reserved
ISBN : 9798356170904

Acknowledgements

The friend Raphaël Loison translates. Here, I thank him for his translation in English. Raphaël translates with inspiration all my poems. And he translated this book in English. Thank you my friend…

Publisher's caveat

The affective ambivalence of the individual ties itself in a perpetual internal conflict of his desire. This internal war is as weighing and difficult to live as it is to explain, understand and accept it...

Hence, the part 1 may sometimes seem stodgy, even if the author preserves the clarity at most. So we hope that the reader will have the wise patience to understand the complex philosophical and psychoanalytical concepts that decipher the inhuman part in Man.

The parts 2 & 3 simplify this theoretical analysis by examples taken in the contemporary society and art. The choice to read only these two parts does not affect the general understanding, but does diminish the meaning in depth.

The inhuman or war within Man

Acknowledgements 5
Publisher's caveat 7

Introduction 15

Part 1 – The individual's affective ambivalence:
    perpetual intimate conflict of desire 17

I – About the human 17

   § 1 – Language is the human humus
   § 2 – The vacuum
   § 3 – Morality

II – About the inhuman 20

   § 1 – Man is a wolf to Man
   § 2 – The death drive
   § 3 – The Culture

III – The law of opposites and ambivalence:
     the positive impact of negative 26

   § 1 – From the law of opposites
        to the law of ambivalence
   § 2 – The two references to language
   § 3 – Developing the power of the being

Partie 2 – Contemporary impact of human ambivalence: a society without father 33

I – The tyranny of abusive narcissism 33

§ 1 – About 'the inhuman' of the contemporary subject
§ 2 – Mutation of the social fabric: the unbearable position of exception
§ 3 – Contemporary consequence: the degraded orality

II – The fragmented Man and the consequences 38

§ 1 – Fragmented system
§ 2 – Loss of the global vision
§ 3 – Destruction of conviviality and mutual aid

III – From the death drive of a brutal financial capitalism to live together 40

§ 1 – Money for money
§ 2 – From the simplification of reality to computation
§ 3 – What is the meaning of '*living together*'?

Partie 3 – Art as a sublimated synthesis of human ambivalence 49

I – Goya, the *"disenchanter"*: the dark background of Human 49

§ 1 – Graphic indictment against the inhuman in Man
§ 2 – *Los Caprichos* (1799)
§ 3 – *The disasters of war* (1810-1820)

II – *The Confusions of Young Törless* sense fascism 61

§ 1 – Abstract of Robert Musil's novel
§ 2 – Archetype of a dehumanization
§ 3 – A mob of three "without-other" at the beginning of the 20th century

III – *Guernica* : painting History and the inhuman in Man 69

§ 1 – Drawing and color: weapons against the war
§ 2 – Premonition of barbary
§ 3 – A History Painting

Conclusion 79

Bibliographical references & Pictures 83

About the author 91

Numbers in parentheses send to the **bibliographical references and pictures** at the end of the volume.

"Human, all too human, (...) is the commemorative monument of a crisis (...) where you see ideal things, I do see... human things, alas! All too human! (...) It seems that a certain aristocratic tasting 'intellectualism' endeavors constantly to overcome a stream of passion that rumbles underneath (1).

At once Nietzsche's "*too human*" seems to suggest some non human. Three words – *inhuman in Man* – three keys linked together and... the preposition 'in', in the center, that points to some inhuman inside and an internal duality. As split by a schism, Man is in a perpetual war between Good and Evil. This intimate and moral breach parts him in two opposite inclinations. This "*affective ambivalence*" (2) (2 bis) emerges from the pair human-inhuman that cuts across him eternally in the form of a conflict of desire. What does this mean?...
(Part 1).

Private to each individual, this divorce reveals itself within the social balance which, thereupon, proves to be always precarious. Does not a fatherless society appear today, threatened by the death drive while it calls for life?
(Part 2).

Art also includes this human dualism: for example, Francisco Goya, Robert Musil and Pablo Picasso unravel it pertinently. Some works actually provide a sublime synthesis of our ambivalence
(Part 3).

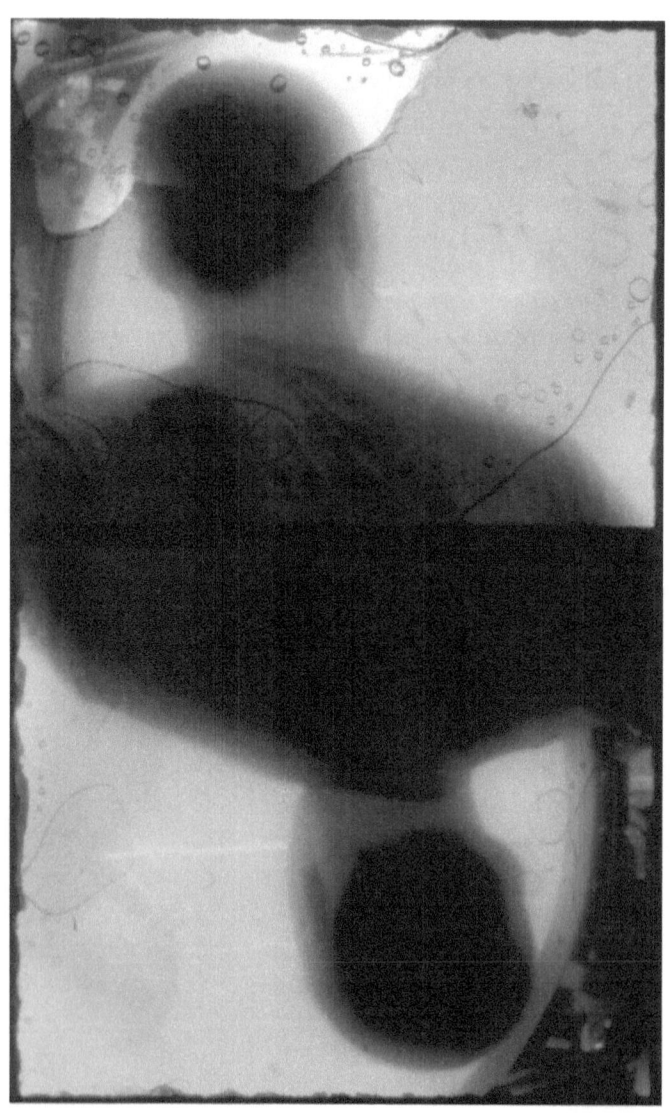

Part 1 – The individual's affective ambivalence: perpetual intimate conflict of desire

Before the dual dynamics (III), the inhuman (II) in Man implies his humanity (I). Man, as a matter of fact, sails between language (§ 1), vacuum (§ 2) and morality (§ 3).

I – About the human

§ 1 – Language is the human humus

Language institutes every man, as Freud means it in *Totem and taboo* (33) (in II-§ 3). For his part, Jacques Lacan – discussing the symbol as the symbolic – continues: "*so the man speaks, but it is because the symbol made him man*" (4). Speech constitutes the human, himself happened thanks to the speech of an other. The non-speech is nature. The speech is culture. By the act of saying and its effects, the symbol holds the power of meaning, and of naming somebody to somebody. "*The role of language is not to inform; it is to invoke*" (4). And... The language makes the "*human humus*" (3) in the condition that this speech does not establish a coercive power but rather a language that creates and protects the equality and the liberty of the members of a Society.
God, Chief, King, President, father, etc. Briefly, these figures that embody a place of exception in the face of the community are not supposed to exert coercion since the speech is their predominant authority. Their power of conviction overcomes their physical force. Their symbolic role does not mean to give orders but to remind to people the laws of the Community. By the means of language they are also in charge of appeasing discords between people.
But, To Speak is a way to accept a loss of pleasure. As a matter of fact, there is a fundamental vacuum in speech.

§ 2 – The vacuum

In 1974, Lacan reintroduces the dimension of drive and its scope in speech with the word "*parlêtre*" (speaking-being / being-speech): "*the carnal being devastated by language who speaks this thing (…) who, strictly speaking, is only up to [thelanguage] *, that is the being*" (5) (5bis). Language constitutes the central anthropological invariant and to speak ensures the humanization. Through the castration's ordeal, education represents the guardian of balance between the collective and the individual.

In an unpublished seminar on January 5th 1966 (6), Lacan establishes the *a Object* (7), singular and unutterable, in its relation with the world of objects. This *a Object* forms an intermediate element since it gives, by comparison, "*truth value*" (7) to the rest of the objects. Its major characteristic is the fault and this fault of the native and inhibited *Thing* is applied to multiple replacing objects whose none ever fully satisfies… love life for example.

Jacques Lacan sums up the *a object*: "*it is no being; that is what vacuum is implied in a request. It is the substitute of the Other, under the form of the object of desire*" (8).

It constitutes the very ethics of the truth of the being, by a kind of attachment to this shortcoming. Thus, the objects of the world are all marked by frustration. What connects human beings and arranges the social bond is a vacuum, a native shortcoming common to all: the *a Object*.

This shortcoming to be, that there is to accept and impossible to transform into symbol, meets morality, essential to Kant.

---

* In 1971, Jacques Lacan contracts "the language" into "**thelanguage**" and by this neologism names **the language of the unconscious** (Also note 5 bis).

§ 3 – Morality

The quality of human also comes from a 'moral', that is what is valued with humanity. To respect the human species in general, human beings as individuals, and to preserve the values usually accepted, all this concerns the quality of human. Because of that, the human quality – by this link to morality – recognizes a value-based judgement. Three propositions of the philosopher Emmanuel Kant back up the duality human-inhuman.

His *Groundwork of the Metaphysic of Morals* (9) establishes three moral necessities:

the first approach considers the action towards the other, by duty and by sensitive inclination, such as sympathy. Then, Man considers himself not as the medium of our own enjoyment but as the aim of our action.

With the second necessity, the human aspect of an act – its moral scope – originates in the "*principle of will*" (9), and not in its effects or in its goals. And so, the issue is to conceive men as sensible individuals, provided with conscience, will and sense. One has to forsake any violent action against them and prefer the law.

As a consequence of the two other propositions, Kant infers the third approach: "*The duty is the necessity to accomplish an act by respect of the law*" (9). In contrast with objects, relative, tradable and provided with a price, Man, considered with "*pure respect*" (9), acquires a singular, unique and absolute value.

The action of his "*good will*" (9), or moral will, obeys not to a sensitive or natural inclination, but to the order expressed by reason, in pure intention. Kant specifies "*the representation of law (…) can only take place within the being provided with reason*" (9).

However only the individual, in his intimacy, knows the base of his action. The Utopia – place without a location – of a human without inhuman is an impossible dream, for Man also harbors an underground world.

II – About the inhuman

Desire is at the origin of everlasting conflicts: "*homo homini lupus est*"! (§ 1). Sigmund Freud locates the inhuman within Man as the crucial element of psychoanalysis, along with the death drive (§ 2) and culture (§ 3).

§ 1 – Man is a wolf to Man

Man is also the worst enemy of his own species. The representation of an inhuman part in Man runs historically with this saying from Plautus to Sigmund Freud.

As a matter of fact, if Michel de Montaigne (10) considers the anthropophagic Tupinamba Indians of Brazil more innocent than men of the socialized state, some others consider them as wolves.

Long before Sigmund Freud, Plautus, already in a story between a father and a son: *Asinaria* (11), first declares by Mercator's mouth: "*When one does not know him, man is a wolf to man*" (11).

In the XVIth century, Erasmus (12) and François Rabelais (13) quote this saying. In the same time, as an advocate of Protestantism, the poet Theodor Agrippa d'Aubigné also mentions the maxim, figuring "*The Tragics*" (14) men as wolves to Man... His great poem indeed depicts the allegory of France as a "*distressed mother*" (14), seeing her sons tearing themselves apart. In his poem, the breast milk merges with blood: "*You stained with blood the breast that nourishes you*" (line 31-32) and "*I only have blood left to nourish you*" (line 34) (14).

The wars of religion demonstrate the very example of the violence of a fight between brothers and of the savagery's resurgence within French civilization.
The forerunner of empiricism, the English philosopher Francis Bacon reports the formula in his major work: *Novum Organum* (15).

Likewise, twenty-two years later, the English philosopher Thomas Hobbes uses it in *De cive* (16) : the civil society frees itself of the wolf's natural savagery in the form of a contract between men in the unity of power.

In the XIXth century, Arthur Schopenhauer in *The World as Will and Representation* (17) and, lastly, Sigmund Freud in 1930, top the inhuman in man with this locution. *Civilization and its discontents* (18) uncovers the evil, the perversion and the selfishness of human nature tempted by the almighty power, at the expense of other: "*a strong amount of aggressivity*" (18) nestles in the human and... the name of the father establishes the Law.

Thus, the philosophic and optimistic vision of Man as a "noble savage", by Montaigne (10) and Rousseau (19) (20), meets the "*homo homini lupus est*" in the Freudian representation disillusioned with human nature. Seneca, for his part, claims: "*Man is a sacred thing for Man*" (21).

In full contrast, disenchanting Freud uncovers in Man, among his three narcissistic wounds * (22), the psychological scar of the death drive.

§ 2 – The death drive

Among the nine writings about the death drive : *Beyond the Pleasure Principle* (1920); *Psychoanalysis and theory of libido* (1923); *The Ego and the Id* (1923); *The economic problem of masochism* (1924); *Civilization and its discontents* (1930) (18); *Why war?* (1932); *New seminars of introduction to psychoanalysis* (1933); *The ended analysis and the analysis without end* (1937); *Compendium of psychoanalysis* (1938), three will be discussed (notes 24 à 31).

Between 1920 and 1932, the death drive, in search of the full diminution of tension, consolidates with a major step forward about the inhuman in Man. Between these two dates, *The ego and the Id* (1923) (26) establishes a new psychic scale between two opposite and complementary impulses (Cf. III).

---

* Three narcissistic wounds caused **by science** because the earth is not the center of the universe; **by anthropology** because Man is a descendant of the ape; and **by psychoanalysis** since the ego is not the master of his home…

As a matter of fact, to the questions: *Why war?* (28) and how to divert civilization from war's damages? the psychoanalyst, in front of the physicist Albert Einstein, answers in three points.

First thinking over the pair 'law-violence', the unity creates force, Freud considers the transfer of power towards a larger group, whose identifications (28 bis), through feelings, foster cohesion.

The destruction drive comes first in his metapsychology. Since 1920, *Beyond the Pleasure Principle* (24) already recognizes: "*The death drive becomes destruction drive when it is driven outwards*" (24). This achievement annihilates the attempt to eliminate violence from human nature. Relying on his "*mythological doctrine of impulses*" (28), Freud deciphers the ethnological reality, highlighting the threat of arbitrariness of two powers: State and Church... the latter "*forbids to think*".

Freud finally concludes: "*Everything that promotes Culture's development also works against war*" (28). In this way, *Why war?* harvests a double crop: conceptual and clinical.

Concerning the concept, clearly mentioning the destruction impulse connected to the death drive, Sigmund Freud demonstrates to which extent war "*makes sense as a collective guideline of the death drives*"(31 bis).

For his part, the harvest of facts grows also richer. In fact, since his introduction to "*About the psychoanalysis of war's neurosis*" (32), in 1919, the part of war in traumas is undeniable.

The following year "*Beyond the Pleasure Principle*" (24) sheds light on the death drive. And, twelve years later, "*Why war?*" (28) generates a major clinical contribution: the state of war allows the use of death drive. However, Sigmund Freud states only indirectly this clinical lesson and maintains his discourse about war's role in Culture.

After a concrete study of politics and history, "*Why war?*" objects thus: the death drive is proven to be the ultimate cause of war by its propensity to generate aggressiveness in the collective. In this way, this open letter questions Culture: its beginning and its function.

§ 3 – The Culture

"*In the beginning was the act*" (33) of the first father's murder: "*One day, the banished brothers united, killed and ate the father, which terminated the existence of the paternal horde*" (33).

Totem and Taboo (33) unveils a civilization of murder, between inhuman relations of a primitive horde and human relationships in a society. After the collective assassination, hate bonds as brothers the men who were before submitted to the tyranny of the wild father. Thus, civilization comes into being with the paternal metaphor. Freud introduces the father at the base of the Law. To become a socialized human necessitates the step of the murder of the limitless archaic father, driven by an inhuman almighty power and the desire of incest. In contrast, the symbolic father is found through speech, relays it and submits to the law of castration.

As a matter of fact, to inhibit the primordial hate in Man – the inhuman underground of generations of murderers – is a role of culture. The human being and culture are based on an initial experience of disgust, and are structured by the constant rejection of an initial evil. Civilization is an eternally upset process, aiming to create a peaceful society whose ideal is a prototype imagined, but never realized. The primeval time evolves towards a historical time, through an act, admittedly murderous, but achieved in a collective manner: "*from a state of nature to a state of Law where the Law is incarnated by the one who, living, figured the total arbitrariness*" (34).

The new world grows less as a universe of force but rather a human alliance where fraternity remains precarious but does exist. In that sense, the collective murder, founder of the society, clarifies social organization as a "*pass line between nature and culture*" (34) – the taboo of incest (33 bis) – the solution to give birth to humanity. From now on, Law and desire are connected. Individual and society as well come from this common repression.

Surely, this constraint inhibits but also gives the framework of Law. The incest's inhibition is a double bond because speech and real life connect with the repressed. The symbolic civilizes Man thanks to this restraint. In the depths of Culture castration and pleasure are hidden. On the surface, the father is projected in destiny which the individual enjoys in castration: "*One enjoys power only as castrated!*" (35). In other words, civilization offers an obstacle to full enjoyment: to get pleasure from Culture triggers punishment...

Thus, the state's power claims for the sacrifice of impulses without offering, or rarely, a counterbalance: the state keeps the exclusivity of injustice and violence…
To avoid discord, Culture represses the ancestral hate and the desire of incest.

Man is split by the internal duality of an affective ambivalence. But this eternal and secret battle of his desire opens itself to the dynamics of contrasts; in other words, in this intimate conflict a positive arises from the negative (III).

III – The law of opposites and ambivalence: the positive impact of negative

From Heraclitus to Freud, this dualism reveals itself as a human law (§1) bolstered by the two bases of language (§2); the two modes, father and mother combined, activate the strength of being in Man including his own death and war as necessary to this dual dynamics (§3).

§ 1 – From the law of opposites to the law of ambivalence

Early in history, Heraclitus questions time and change, the constant and the temporary. Death, unconceivable, appears inexpressible. Relying on sensitive datas, the only remaining element in change is change itself: and so, no permanence, everything changes. A principle of opposites rules the universe and rallies them constantly: *polemos*.

Harmony occurs through *polemos*, between the opposite stresses, so far as these opposites produce the equilibrium when passed over. Inseparable, opposites hold in themselves their existence and their mobility by their contrast (God-men; poor-rich; woman-man, etc).

Developing little about the *polemos*, Freud however establishes a law of ambivalence: in 1923, articulated with the death drive, his new topic (1) clarifies the dynamics of the psyche in the form of conflict. As if 'alienated', the ego finds itself "*in a bond of dependance*" (26) in two new keys: the Id and the Superego. In its weakness, but constant, the ego tries to preserve itself by the union of the two opposite and complementary authorities.

The Dostoïevski case (1928) (36) brings out the thin link between the superego and the feeling of guilt through the Oedipus complex: the little boy, wanting his father's death, punishes himself by guilt. In reference to *Totem and Taboo* (1913) – in the ambiguity between the idea of the neurotic and the action of the primal man – two contrary and bonded affects arise, love and hate – channeling towards the father in confluence – founding a genealogy of Civilization by this very murder.

In fact, parricide constitutes the major origin of guilt, in an ambivalence of feeling, between the hate of the rival and the tenderness for him: "*under the effect of the castration's anguish, and so in the interest of preserving his manhood, he will give up the desire to possess the mother and to eliminate the father*" (36). Thus, as an originating language, the father's Law structures Man with the taboo of incest.

§ 2 – The two references to language

So, the affective ambivalence originates in the references to language with two modes of psychic economics.

The first language is the mother's order. This language coincides with *the Thing* (See the graphic below), the body, the almighty power, the immediate, the reciprocity, the mirror, the same and the full. In this regime there is a matching between the word and the *das Ding* (In German, the thing) of the philosopher Heidegger (37bis). An earthen container is, at the same time, material and content. The clay is the real thing but the liquid contained by the vase is the *Thing*… and this *Thing* depicts the essence of the object… the matrix of the individual representations.

Summary of *The Thing* which includes the "a Object"
Lacan's *The Thing* coordinates itself around 5 elements: 1/the Subject who desires 2/empirical objects; but 3/a Mystery rises because in him 4/a lack is born. Hence the intervention of 5/the "*a Object*" that channels the impulse of the subject towards desired objects, always looked for outside, but… never really satisfying.

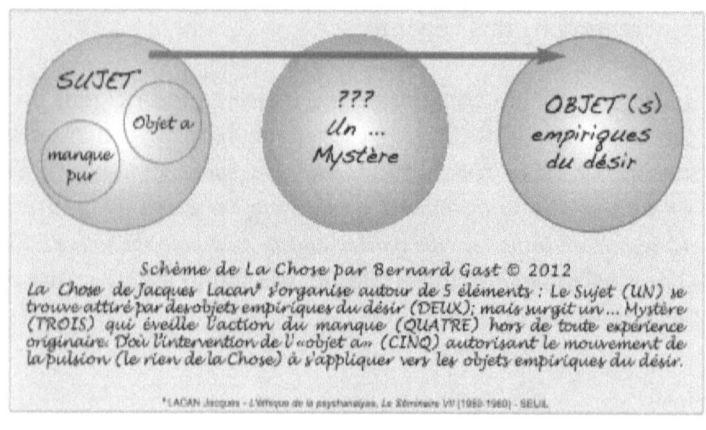

The second 'language' is the Law of the father. This language coincides with the word, the asymmetry, the deficit enshrined in the language, the vacuum, the loss and the fault. There, the word and *the Thing* are revealed as unfit.

These two references to language that produce human psyche animate every individual in a personal manner.

But society experiences "*a progress of civilization*" (37) if the symbolic role of the father-mode regulates the mother-mode "*because maternity is certified by the evidence of perception when paternity is a speculation, (is) based on a deduction and a postulate*" (37).

Between the mother-mode and the father-mode the conflict of an equivocal desire runs from *the Thing* to the speech.

Caught between reality and language, this arranged dual system of psychic economics regulates the socialized Man according to two cornerstones.

ONE, *the Thing* as the "object of the incest" that figures the mother with her fundamental characteristic of fulfilling the role of *the Thing*, entity-object that escapes every Human.

And,

TWO, the incest assimilated to the most essential desire but… prohibited. As a matter of fact, a veil comes down over incest as the excluded desire because, in fact, essentially central… this unconscious, unforgettable, lost object – incessantly desired, searched outside – but unattainable…

Sigmund Freud flips the ethical law insofar as the courted supreme Good, the Mother, is an interdict nevertheless figuring the only good : *"the Sovereign Good, which is das Ding, which is the Mother, the subject-matter of the incest, is a forbidden good, and there is no other good. Such is, for Freud, the reversed foundation of the moral law"* (38).

The taboo of incest forms the necessary basis for the maintenance of speech. In the unconscious, *the Thing* (39) imposes its law. And without being the Law, *the Thing* gets known by the Law, for the interdict of the Law makes us want *the Thing*. Desire ignites from the forbidden link with the Law, and so becoming desire of death: a transgression *"above the moral, an eroticism"* (38).

§ 3 – Developing the power of the being

Culture, based on speech, thus forbids total enjoyment, while fostering living together. However, the troubles, eventually induced by the repression of 'inhuman' impulses, leads education into a dialectic between the body's exuberant powers and the speech's forces. Then, a singular path of humanity may be traced from impulse to desire. But, in dual dynamics, the power to be develops itself in a link with the meditation about death and… war. Although, concerning directly the structure of human, the negative nature of death refers, the other and oneself, to the inconceivable, in an ambiguous attitude towards death. The death anxiety comes, for example, from the guilt of having wished somebody's death. *"If you want to be able to bear life, be ready to accept death"* (40): Internalize death helps to tolerate life.

From the positive perspective of the negative, an ideology considers war as a necessity. Through the breaking of individualism war builds the collective. From sacrifice arise the superior values. Through the work of test, the individual emerges from withdrawal, channels himself towards the essential of being and finds a meaning to death, in front of death. War prepares peace.

Still, despite the economic war, today a comeback of the barbary may be seen – like a search of the power to be by the possession, power of having – a crisis of peace by war and pleasure at any cost. To see the positive of negative proves to be quite hard…

In front of the diptych *Nature-Impulse-Sexuality* and *Culture-Language-Art*, the repressed almighty power succeeds, through the destructive face of Narcissus. This intimate split displays its effects on civilization through a fragile stability, always to be supported.

Today shows the inhumanity of an abusive narcissism's tyranny (I). This excess of the mother mode, at the expense of the father mode, haunts culture by partitioning Man (II), surrounded by a violent capitalism, while calling him to think living together over (III).

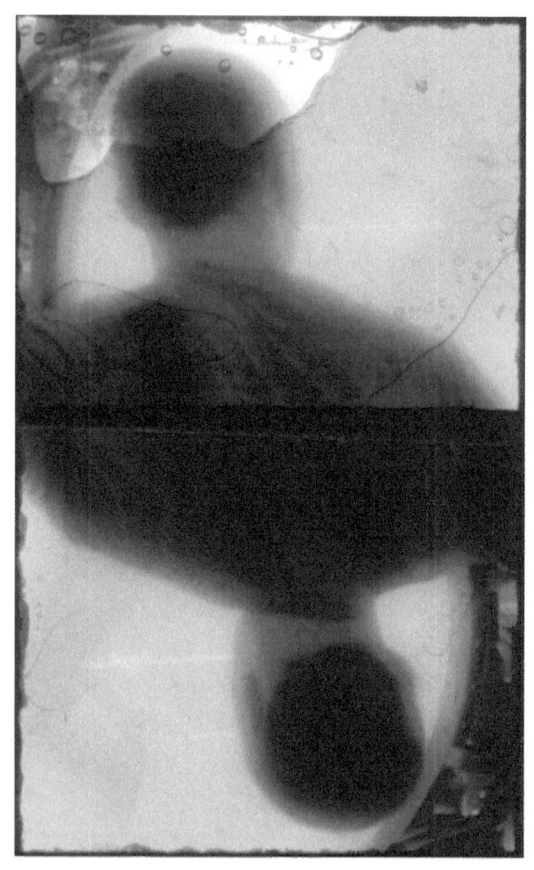

Part 2 – Contemporary impact of human ambivalence: a society without father

I – The tyranny of abusive narcissism

The contemporary society positions the individual in front of the scenery of an enjoyment without constraint. Paradoxically with the forgetfulness of death, the logic of death of a perverse culture is implemented. In this XXIst century's beginning a "*new psychic economics*" (43) of the social bond and the subject is unveiled.

This "*neo-subject*" is a "*man without seriousness*" (42) whose 'inhumanity' is highlighted by three clues: his loss of the symbolic, his refusal of the father 's Law and of the encounter (§ 1). A mutation of the social fabric (§ 2) comes from this helplessness to accept the father's Law and disastrous backlashes such as addiction (§ 3).

§ 1 – About 'the inhuman' of the contemporary subject

ONE – Today, the mother mode overpowers the father mode. Indeed, without past's landmarks, the neo-subject organizes and builds alone the social fabric from his own umbilicus. But, become a neo-Atlas of a self-created world – without knowing it, porter of the burden of the whole social group – he confronts himself to his powerlessness with the consequences of addiction, depression, abdication or suffocation. He suffocates by lack of reality, while living the reality from then on as a wound to heal of. To exempt himself from this reality, necessarily painful, this neo-subject shifts away from language for action... sometimes violent.

Yet, his violence is not vertical anymore – in a relation of constraints with a "*place of exception*" (41) – forcing him to convert his aggressiveness in another attitude. Without a higher target of exception and without a consistent protagonist, his violence is horizontal, expressed against the other, against himself, or both. This tragic child of nobody suffers an un-filiation: for lack of a solid referral to clash swords with, he fights a kind of nothing. Not at all deconstructed but more unable to build, without anybody to convey him the renunciation's obligation, this neo-pseudo-subject ignores the necessity of sacrifice to give a value to his acts.

TWO – When the repression concerns normal neurosis, denial and disclaimer concern a new form of perversion: "*ordinary perversion*" (41). The psychoanalysts' practices do not get full of classical neurosis but more of this ordinary perversion through which the neo-subject seeks to avoid structuration. Keeping the phallus away and so the relation to the father. Not finding his place in the father mode, he runs after recognition without a solid base.

Through his refusal to lose any inch of pleasure, he denies any castrating and building paternal antecedent. This neo-subject gets entangled in the Great Mother of optimal enjoyment and oversized confusion; in other words, in a collective perversion and not at all an individual perversion.

This perverse economics frees itself from the symbolic, and so from the shortage. However, this vacuum builds the social and the singular parts of the subject. But in order to consent this loss of enjoyment, a father figure must assume the responsibility of this loss. Yet, this figure of authority is untenable in a society of "*without-other*" (41).

THREE – In defense, the "*without-other*" is subjected, without his knowledge, by the collective perversion of the system (See later in II & III)... Deprived of a relationship to the real father entrusted to push him out of the nest, the relationship to the mother overpowers him and his relationship to the object of desire eludes the paternal castration. As a "*subject of limbo*" (44) (in Latin *limbus*: on the edge of the other's threshold) he avoids the encounter. This "*without-other*" of a confined world pursues a goal that stops him from entering in relation with the other: hence his solitude. In 1967, Michel Tournier writes "*Friday or the other island*" (45). Gilles Deleuze sees there a pervert learning a life without an other. Robinson loses speech and the reference of words, these lighthouses of humanity. He also loses the other because he loses his humanity. This pervert – ordinary but non structural - does not meet the other anymore. Ergo, this neo-subject destroys in himself the authority of the other: *(…) The pervert's world is a world without an other, and so a world without possibilities*" (41).

The contemporary transformation of the social bond leads to the death of the other because the link with the real other decreases increasingly. The limitation to the anthropological structure that the carnal perception of the real father may bring at the heart of the mind will decrease accordingly to this perception's decline.

In front of the death of a sacred paternal order – arising with the great confusion and the mainstreamed child – the lack of maturation of some psychic forms requires to "*implement a practice other than analysis, a practice that, however, will converge with it in its intention*" (46).

§ 2 – Mutation of the social fabric :
   the unbearable position of exception

Is the notion of hierarchy – of sacred order – nowadays obsolete? Does the empty sky of God's death command to create a new space of transcendence without transcendence? The danger – menacing the subject and the society – calls for a jurisdiction of substitution.

Even the transfer of the transcendent legitimacy from religion to state – in its secular form – unveils the weakness of the status of chief, king, father, master, teacher, etc. Is an authority of love inadmissible? Is a power that loves but sets limits unacceptable? Every "*place of exception*" is untenable. A crisis of validity concerns now the society as a whole: politics, teaching, government.

As a matter of fact, the hypermodernity swaps in a radical way the position of the Other. This anthropological reversal may be summed up as a transition from a religious society where the subject if a child of God, followed by a scientific boom where the subject is a child of science, to reach the hypermodern society and its violent liberalism where the subject is a child of nobody. The subjective and social mutation gives form to an unconscious permutation from "*a neurotic economics to a perverse economics where castration is impossible*" (47).

And yes, for years, the patients in our practices express more a new manner of perversion than 'the good old neurosis' of the origins…

And in spite of this… it is essential to allow a space to the Other, despite the non-desire to give him this space... As early as 1968, Jacques Lacan and his *"generalized child"* (48) presages this contemporary world where the infantile almighty power rules.

Nevertheless, to become a subject and a being of speech forces to lose. The illusion of omnipotence, the remoteness of reality, the contestation of social engendering draw the picture of social dereliction. The individual exists through the social bond; yet the contemporary subject, reversing the reality, imagines that this social bond exists because he exists.

Rejecting its filiation to the previous community, this mainstreamed child declines his debt to society: the social past is no longer a reference point. It remains only a utilitarian function of the collective. Those new social subjects satisfy themselves by activating themselves in total harmony; recognizing themselves and each other, exclusively for the only necessity, not chosen, to belong to the collective.

A more or less conscious way to express: *"I make use of the social bond but it won't make use of me!"*.

§ 3 – Contemporary consequence: the degraded orality

The linguist Jean Szlamowicz wrote about sheep-like thinking (49). Aren't we thinking like sheep when speech weakens, denounces and divides?

A devaluated speech is as hollow as baseless thought, or even does not respect what it enounces. Political speech is a current example but disfigured speech is displayed in other places… Under radical and often void formulations an absence of scientific rigor hides behind an appearance of depth.

Danger rises from an ideology that manipulates by altering language. Does not a dividing culture eradicate what brings humans together? Thus, does *Woke* culture seek really a universal culture through a multiform language (Queer, gender, inclusivism, etc.)?

In the illusion of everything possible and the rejection of the debt to the other, these "*without-other*" lose their humanity, living together without the other who happens to be sacrificed.

From this follows the addiction of every kind. Indeed, turned into a social symptom, the object, not used to speak to anymore but to consume, leads to the degraded orality of the fractured Man.

II – The fragmented Man and the consequences

So, the overall-pleasure overpowers the desire of the "without-other", entangled in a mother-mode without boundaries. As a matter of fact, today shows the germination of a divided human, often isolated (§ 1 et § 3) and deprived of a complete and universal vision (§ 2).

§ 1 – Fragmented system

The first symptom is the fragmentation of the system: the sociality takes the form of fragmentation, not just of knowledge, but also of individuals. The contemporary sociality invents division. For example, medicine fragments Man within a world of specialists. The bureaucratization isolates each one within his segment. Ultimately, the relation to time is also divided: harassed by time, the watch, the mobile phone warning incessantly of the loss of time and commands to save time. A generalized frenzy follows in a society submitted to the gross national product.

§ 2 – Loss of the global vision

A logic of specialization encloses each one, isolated in one's segment, growing unable to grasp the global system. Learned very early in school, this partitioned mode of thought, isolating the objects, prevents the links between them : to know many things in detail, but isolated, ignores the whole. Divided knowledge – ignoring the links – creates a new ignorance of the other and of sociality.

§ 3 – Destruction of conviviality and mutual aid

The inhumanity in human relationships also sticks out in the destruction of conviviality, however essential to Man. Those consequences dictate a new thinking of the human complexity, the social complexity and… the future of man.

III – From the death drive of a brutal financial capitalism to live together

Seeking to fill his shortage by the consummation of objects, in every sense of the word, this fragmented Man faces the reign of money for money (§ 1). An excessive capitalism activates inhuman effects by a simplification of reality through computation (§ 2). And so much death drive commands the rise of a new way of living in community (§ 3).

§ 1 – Money for money

Today, money, as a social symptom, hands over Man to an inhuman capitalism. Greed, the addiction to money, kills folks and civilizations. By its greedy confusion capitalism diverts and changes a means, the capital, into an end. A dogma off reality imposes itself: the role of economy and enterprises is to maximize the stockholders' patrimony. Yet, an enterprise works only in respect of often complex and delicate equilibriums. With this doctrine, greed becomes the basic rule of economical functioning. *Avida Dollars* * rules!

* Anagram of Salvador Dali found by André Breton

A feeling of individual fault intensifies this evil. Man is responsible for the reason that he acts. Not only he is stuck in a traffic jam, he himself is a jam. Impossible to exonerate oneself because every one finds oneself accomplice and belonging to the system. In fact, to invent a new future comes to mind.

A specific temptation of the father – preoccupied by his own survival – consists of not transmitting or wrongly transmitting, the symbolic speech to his offspring. This father is not a symbolic father any more but a wild father. But, in reality, the social symptoms unveil also the bitter crop of choices made by the previous generations. The contemporary difficulty of transmission comes also from realities. For example, today, the ultimate beneficiaries of the financial capitalism are the money savers of western democracies: those, having worked during the "*Glorious Thirty*" (1945-1975), are retired or soon to be. However, the returns required by the financial markets on the physical economy (real) benefit to these same savers. How does the created value get shared between generations? Or, rather, how, in full conscience (as it is trendy to say), do the generations accept to share what is needed tomorrow in order to live together? This generational fracture – embraced in the reality – invites to think together what concerns everyone and to share with the younger generations for a more harmonious future. The father from the "*Glorious Thirty*", even if he provides a symbolic transmission to his children – also conveys his social knowledge now obsolete and so different from the society of today's generations... Yet, this pernicious model of money for money – reducing reality to computation – leads to multiple pervert impacts to Man.

§ 2 – From the simplification of reality to computation

Simplifying the reality to only a few agents does increase profit. But this simplification launches fateful consequences: unemployment, isolation, marginalization, psycho-social risks, etc.

Social death lurks with violent backlashes… as in 1994, when Erick Schmidt, unemployed, is killed by the police because he took children as hostages against ransom. Who is responsible? Society, as an organization without any moral conscience or its own will? Does the fault lie with the free individual? Or is his act the "*expression of the fight for positions that rages in our world*"? The "*fight for positions*" (50) is the fight of socially isolated beings, seeking a position which is a social existence and an identity in the same time.

By imposing a monopoly the mass-market retailing simplifies, perhaps reduces, the reality to a few agents. The disappearance of small shops, craftmanship and convivial organizations. This other example of the fight for positions – between multinational companies of agro-food industry and small farmers – encourages to reconsider activities so that a maximum of economic agents would be actors of the economy and not a unique monopole. As a matter of fact, the monopole, a form of the death drive, big devourer of human beings, excludes and wipes the figure of the other out. Should not this process be changed since its negative effects are far more important than the positive ones?

In fact, the industrial and digital civilization applies industry and digitalization to sectors where its mode proves to be pervert and remote from life. Finally, is not bio agriculture a return to life, producing without destroying? In contrast, synthetic pesticides destroy the environment, contaminate waters… "*Soon, before eating, one will have to wish good luck rather than good appetite!*" (51). The logic of profit prevails by spoiling and wrecking. The contemporary world splits Man up for profit. The civilization shows in this way its ambivalence – producing through destruction, without limits and without goal – overwhelmed by the narrow and limited knowledge of… computation.

As a consequence, two dangers currently afflict Culture. On one hand, the almighty power of intolerant thinking witnesses the aggravation of the various forms of fanaticism (religious, national, etc.); on the other hand, the tyranny of financial capitalism, seeking unlimited profit, maintains the rule of rivalry. Everywhere, in a more or less underground way, greed and money prevail.

Is there no place for a civilization in which profit would not be the essential share? No place for a culture where personal life, cost-freedom, endowment, mutual aid, solidarity would be important? The decay of all these elements of western contemporary civilization unveils the fundamental issue whose industrialization, digitalization and agriculture are just aspects. Behind so much death at work in individuals and in sociality, a healthy return to the main question is crucial: what does living together mean?

§ 3 – What is the meaning of living together?

To reconsider this logic of death by rethinking the relation to Earth and to Life. The Earth feeds Man and Man poisons Earth. Man poisons himself! The positive side of the negative quality of this death drive is to force to question oneself about the meaning of Life: in the end, what is living? Even before knowing if there is a life after death, is there a life before death?

In the most complete illusion Man finds himself embedded in a system that makes him dependent. There he is enslaved by the tools he created. Tools to serve him admittedly… The industrial and digital miracle is also a nightmare. How fragile is this culture! Without connections, fuel and electricity the individual and collective human system collapses.

Man is divorcing from the very bases of Nature. In this way, modern agriculture achieves production through destruction, are there no limits to indefinitely produce and destroy? Looking at the evaluation over human and animal health or water, etc.? What meaning of life does Man consider? Which kind of living together? Without the objective and the set in motion of a bonded, convivial and peaceful humanity, civilization is quite useless. Yet, globalization maintains profit rivalry as a game rule: to sell-to buy!

Humans have to regain a serenity, allowing a living-together at last more livable. In spite of the affective duality written in Man and the civilization built upon a murder, this logic leading to death behaviors has to be questioned.

Still, unfortunately it is not incompatible to produce and eat bio, to recycle one's water, to use solar energy and... to exploit one's neighbors.

Which future for humanity does Man want? And upon which values to build a western and planetary living-together? For the question is not only a western one and nor secondary for starving humans on the fringes of the future... Today, a common future must be envisioned in the perspective of edifying a soothed human kind... Respectful of the fundaments of Life.

For example, agrobiology turns out to be not only able to handle and solve world hunger but also to bring back life in deserted countrysides. With contemporary culture the difference between life and survival emerges. Survival forces to earn one's living without joy, to make a living through its loss. To live should mean flourishing; to live lies in the community and the flourishing of Man.

Life is love and tenderness. But computation ignores life and calculates everything. Computation is unable to calculate love and hate. Computation calculates objects. Computation is unable to calculate feelings. Man lives under this influence through surveys, statistics, etc.
A cybernetic and merchant universe pulls the strings through metaverses* and algorithms...

---

* Metaverse is the contraction of meta and universe. So, the issue is about a virtual universe reaching beyond the material world.

Is the exit of the outrageous financial capitalism the primary solution? Almighty like the generalized child promised by Lacan as early as 1968. This hyper-capitalism, almighty in our days, terrorizes governments and populations by modeling the world.

Is the reimplantation of reality's complexity in the economic machinery the second way out? To industrialize and digitize everything amounts to homogenize and standardize everything... Including Man. Under the tyranny of normality, to be fully individualized looks like a mistake!

How to go towards a new model that regulates quantity while improving quality?
Does not the return to conviviality and interchange tend to be indispensable? With local stores of course but also with generations accepting consciously to share?

Art offers, sometimes, a sublimated synthesis of human affective ambivalence. Masterpieces of art give an authentic vision able to support the contemporary reflection.

Does the black works of Spanish painter Francisco de Goya already suggest today's violent melancholy? Their philosophical satire calls for an altruistic behavior (I).

Does Robert Musil prophesy – thirty-three years in advance – the coming of national-socialism? Does not the moral trouble of Young Törless touch on similarities with the tyranny of today's neo-teenagers' narcissism (II)?

And when Pablo Picasso paints his historic *Guernica*, is not his painting a metaphor of human suffering and of the inhuman in Man (III)?

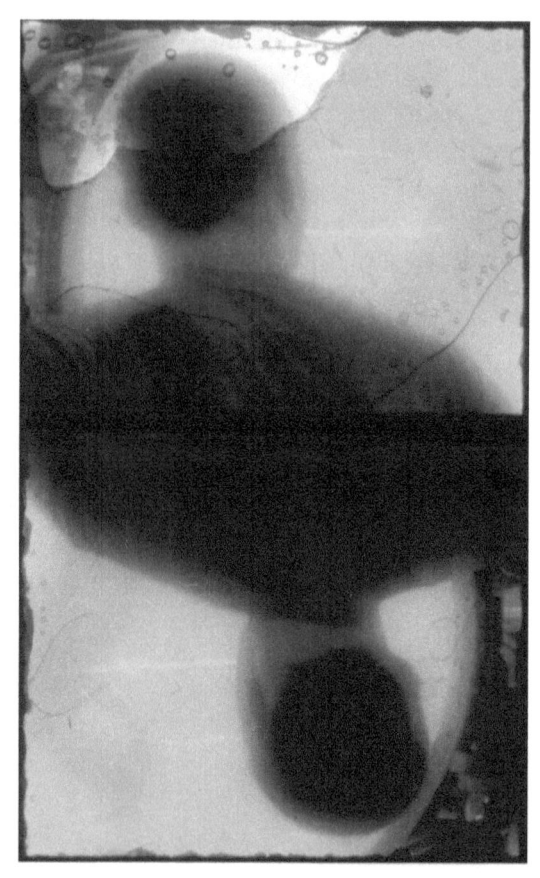

Partie 3 – Art as a sublimated synthesis of human ambivalence

The French Revolution coincides with a *"black romanticism"* (52) which shakes rudely the Society in the whole Europe. In front of terror and wars, the common sense experiences a wreck. Then a few artists explore this feeling of a loss of control in Man. Francisco Goya considers human impulses that challenge human reason.
Firstly, he is interested by the body and its animality through its destructive, dominant and overpowering features. Secondly, Goya's interests go to dreams and insane acts originated from unconscious impulses.

The Spanish artist explores these new fields and frees himself from social and moral norms. Using the age-old popular beliefs, this *"disenchanter"* paints with all the hues of black.

I – Goya, the disenchanter: the dark background of Human

His father is a gilder master. But his son Francisco creates dark etchings – the *Caprichos* (§ 2), the *Disasters of War* (§ 3) – and the *Black Paintings*. From father to son, the artist goes from the spiritual Sky's gold to Human's dark background. The enigma of shadow seems to be his most beautiful pictorial mastery but also philosophical in order to signify the war in Man (§ 1).

§ 1 – Graphic indictment against the inhuman in Man

Goya's fame comes essentially from his painting. His etchings prove to be prominent: as original and significant of his identity and his thinking. The artist literally paints with the aquatint to stage powerful contrasts combined with a large and subtle spectrum of hues. This technique is ideal to reveal the dramatic effects of the affective duality human-inhuman in its entire scale of emotions.

The year he turns 46 (1792) marks an essential milestone of his life : a disease – maybe a meningitis – makes him deaf and weak. The event may probably be one of the sources of his black manner to come. The works realized after his disease correspond to his most authentic style.

The greatest freedom arises from these personal works, so distant from the constraints imposed by commands. And the *Caprichos*, the *Disasters of War* and the *Black Paintings* are not commanded works. The fear of his own death and other evil spirits are expressed in a new approach. Goya's work becomes more profound through a mysterious and blossoming language fueled by the hope of a society reformed by the Enlightment of intellect. However his reflection turns to be more skeptical and closer to a vision black and without ideal. His philosophical evolution is clearly detected in 1799's *Caprichos* (53).

Eighty prints aquatint etchings sketch ironic topics about people of his time. France invades Spain in 1808 and until 1828 the period is a dark one for Spanish people. Francisco Goya is torn apart between his 1789's "French" ideas and his Spanish patriotism.

Between 1810 and 1820, he realizes eighty-two etchings, The *Disasters of War* (54) displaying a wild indictment against Napoleonic violence. These etchings testify the conflict's abomination through sequences of killings, famines, etc. Simultaneously his *Emphatic Caprichos* display his satiric critic of power.

Today's Man's condition may be set sometimes through older ways. Amid the social mutation of 18th century Goya brings to light some obviousness imperceptible to others. Very early, before Nietzsche's writings, he paints and etches the hazard born from the values and the behaviors of an era without transcendence caught in the hopeless coldness of the prominent materiality.

When some others keep on representing the divine by colored skies, Goya chooses the side of disenchantment through the enigma of black.
Is the issue of Being and its abysses guided by the promise of a Sky over Man becoming an illusion to Goya's eyes ?

In any case, Middle Age's luminous and spiritual gold is missing in his figures whose monstrous inside paralyzes the pace. The artist paints their void and emptiness.

As a counterpart to his brightly colored gallant scenes, this alchemist of Art shows the world's dark underside: "*this painter tears apart the ontologically happy depiction, he reaches what one could call a black background – absolutely black, as black as the chasm between the stars*" (55).

§ 2 – *The Caprichos* (1799)

Some of the *Caprichos*' prestige gets minimized by the Inquisition's censorship although *The Caprichos* were royal commands.
Those aquatints are a social satire of the time's Spain, mainly of the Church and aristocracy. This genuine philosophical illustrated book displays a clear criticism against the inhuman in Man: belief, folly, defects, prostitution, corruption, huckster, blindness of the behaviors granted by wealth, power's bias, etc.

Ridicule and nonsense are used to blame human vices and misconducts. The artist's friendship with some Spanish thinkers brings him closer to the Enlightment's ideal in the fight against the Inquisition and for a fair education for all. Francisco de Goya suggests the inhumanity by two graphic and literary techniques: chiaroscuro and double-entendre.

And so, his opinions deepen through the chiaroscuro reinforced by the luminous parts.

To this expressionism of the light he adds his revolution of double-entendre: he writes formulas and/or titles inside the pictures. So, these abrasive critics – often with a double visual and written meaning – suggest a duality in meaning. This dualism arises from the title itself: before being titled *The Caprichos* these etchings are titled *The Dreams*.

Los Suenos (1797), composed of 28 preparatory drawings and 72 etchings, are achieved two years later as *The Caprichos*.

In the two creations the human sinners keep their human appearance, change into sorcerers or pick up some animal features portraying their defects. The art historian Marina Cano Cuesta (56) identifies the origin of the title in Giambatista Tiepolo's *Capricci*, meaning the illusions of reality.

Goya, as well as Freud, is really a disenchanter!

Some imprecision in the titles is evidently a way to hide his moving ahead in order to protect himself from aristocrats and inquisitors. Between living and sailing, already!...

His behavior is ambiguous since he is close to the Enlightment's philosophers and also the official King's painter. Indeed, accused by the Inquisition for the ambiguity of *Capricho* n° 23, (57) he obtains the royal protection by offering *The Caprichos* to the King. Besides the ambiguity of titles, Goya cloaks his discourse by organizing his etchings incoherently.

Though, four obvious themes and a separate group stand out through this disorganization.

The first theme is the caricature of love linked to solicitation and the function of madam. With erotic satire he induces at once the farce of his time. The *Capricho* n° 1 is an ultimate of self-derision where *Francisco de Goya y Lucientes, Painter* shows himself as a dignitary (58).

By etching buffoons the artist lays out the violent and hidden scheming of the court. The social truth shines, the masks being lowered, in the features of a beautiful woman. The caption of the preparatory drawing of the *Capricho n° 6 – No one knows each other (Nadie se conoce) –* summarizes his message: "*The world is a masquerade: face, dress and voice, everything is fake. Each one wants to look what they are not, each one cheats and no one knows each other*" (59).

The witch represents one of the most innovative topics linked to the tragi-comedy of superstition and corresponds to the *Suenos* (Dreams) or *Brujerias* (Witchcrafts). Far from the naturalistic representation of other artists, Goya's work becomes here violently romantic. A universe inhabited by enigmatic and devilish entities conveys the murky inside enshrined in Man. The bodily distortions of witches suggest the malice, the wickedness and, already, the future Freudian death drive. In the print n° 43, *The Sleep of Reason Produces Monsters*, Goya depicts himself surrounded by nightmares and specifies on the preparatory drawing: "*The dreaming author. His intention is only to dissipate the harmful vulgarities and to go on with this work of caprices the strong testimony of the truth.*" (60)

The behavior of clerics provides the third theme of *Duendes* figuring the domestic demons and, by extension in the 18th century, the monks. Goya dresses these characters with clerical outfits. Another mutation may be seen in the *Caprichos*. Innocuous at first, the *Duendes* evolve along the succession of the etchings into mean creatures that become the metaphor of insatiable clerics living at the expense of the people. *"They are hot"*, the *Capricho* n° 13, with an ambiguous title and an expressionist chiaroscuro, focuses on a picture with multiple meanings (61).

In spite of its scarcity, the fourth theme criticizes the Society (education of children, inquisition, unbalanced unions, etc.). The *Caprichos* n° 42 and 63 illustrate a wrongful social organization. The artist's reflection goes from a print to another, from hope to pessimism. *"Thou who cannot"* (n° 42), where two rustic bear two happy donkeys, invokes a policy of class division between idle donkeys (clerics, aristocrats) and the active People supporting idle ones (62). *"Look how solemn they are !"* (n° 63) hardens the statement: the rustic are now donkeys ridden by monsters among which a bird of prey. The agrarian reform is a failure and those enslaved find themselves exploited by the aristocratic and clerical greed (63).

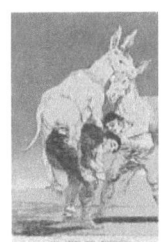

Capricho n° 63   *Capricho n° 42*

The six *Caprichos* (n° 37 to 42) constitute the separate group of the "*Donkeynesses*" and symbolize intellectuals but above all figure human nature's vices in general (64).

Beyond these themes, Goya's *Caprichos* may be organized in two groups. The first forty prints – the sharpest and naturalists – ridicule the behavior of his fellow men relying on rationality. The first half displays mainly the caricature of love. This series discloses the woman's whims in love, her lack of amorous commitment and of compassion for the beloved. This womanhood goes hand in hand with the old madam as the intimate counselor of the feminine Eros.

In contrast, the last forty *Caprichos* forget rationality and are based on nonsense. These phantasmagoric aquatints display an imaginary world of weird creatures. The sequence discredits the social compromises in a truly innovative way.

Goya's style pulls away from the patronizing social satire and turns honest and carnal. The artist restrains himself to dark and enigmatic skits, shams of daily chronicles in strange surroundings. The Spanish engraver distorts outrageously faces and bodies to symbolize stupidity and faults in a wild design.

Image in the *Caprichos* is unquestionably essential but writing is also riveting by its creative and non-dogmatic openness. Besides extremely suggestive titles some formulas broaden the image. These comments, written by Goya himself, summarize his black humored satirical thought. Sometimes the equivocity of a statement suggests a first literal meaning and, by some wit, a second one strongly caricatural. Some other remarks come from contemporary art circles. In this case, several interpretations may occur as about the *Capricho* n° 51, "*They spruce themselves up*" (65) of which three different comments are known.

In the 20th century, the Surrealists who consider the unconscious as the heart of Art see Francisco de Goya, like themselves, as an explorer of dreams. Surrealism undertakes the legacy of Black Romanticism. First, for his unconventional and aesthetic taste for dissonances in which unite farce and transcendence, cruelty and sensuality. Also for his excessiveness. And lastly for the desertion of reason and for the dream that leads to the turmoil of the untamable expressions of the unknown, of the body. By the way, in 1936, the *New-York's International Surrealist Exhibition* (66) displays a few *Caprichos*...

André Malraux (67) sees Goya as one of the artists at the origin of modern art. Away from any moralism, he considers his work being enriched at the deep source of the unconscious.
Breaking away from the gallant and decorative of the king's commands, Francisco de Goya founds a unique style of which *Los Caprichos* draw the oscillation between dream and reality, Human and inhuman of an intimate and imaginary Cinema.

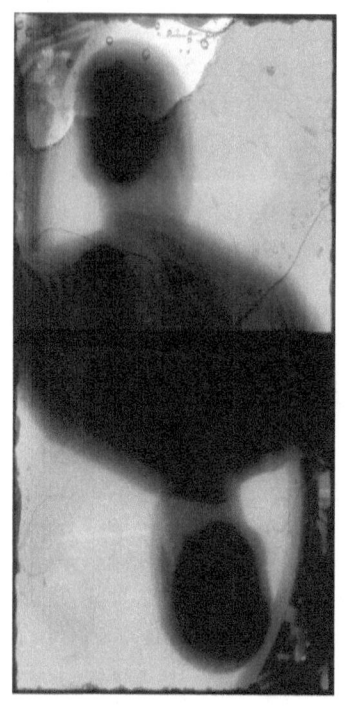

§ 3 – *The Disasters of War* (1810-1820)

In 1808, alleging Portugal's conquest, Napoleon 1st invades Spain. His brother Joseph takes the Spanish crown over the legitimate King, Carlos IV, and his son Ferdinand VII. The Spanish uprising against the invader inaugurates a trying period of the country's history. Undermined by the failure of Russia's campaign, in, 1812, Napoleon's troops withdraw from Spain. In 1813, Ferdinand VII recovers Spain's throne. Distressed by the French occupation, the war and his personal tragedy, Goya carries out, in blood stone, the preparatory drawings for the future etchings of *The Disasters of War* (54). Started in 1810, the series of eighty prints is completed in 1820, under three major themes.

Forty-seven etchings demonstrate the dreadful sequels of war and the cruelties committed by both factions.

Seventeen prints display Francisco Goya's compassion for the sufferings of Spanish people: social disparity and Madrid's great famine.

The last sixteen draw the dark kingship of Ferdinand VII through the establishment of an obscurantist and conservative theocracy: reactionary church, royal absolutism, decadent aristocracy, credulous and ignorant people.

By the end of his life, his creation explores a nothingness very evocative for the contemporary Man... The French Revolution perishes in the Terror; Goya, disabused, doubts Man and paints his anxious and bold *Black Paintings* (1819-1823). *The Dog* (68) dives beyond melancholy. Lucid and cruel, his discernment affirms itself yet without enjoyment. Goya is neither a moralist nor a dupe... but he has compassion for the *Disasters of War* and for the *Caprichos* of Man.

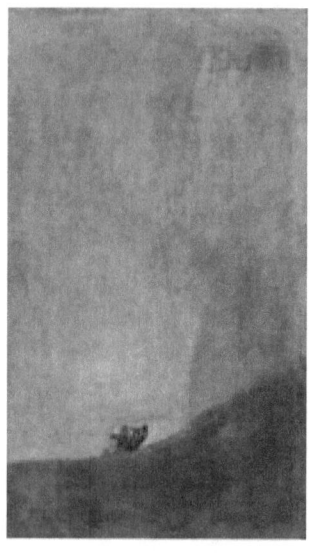

(68) GOYA – *The dog*
(*Peintures noires* : 1819-1823) – Prado, Madrid

By manifesting the affective duality of Man, Francisco de Goya – Pablo Picasso, later – demonstrates the intuitive power of Painting to reveal the truth during a mutation in Culture. Art sometimes listens to the future even before Philosophy. Then, Art becomes the pathfinder of spiritual caution.

In 1906, with his first novel, *The Confusions of Young Törless*, the Austrian Robert Musil (69) displays his intuition of the violence inflicted to Man by the Nazi authoritarian system. In this black and troubled chronicle of an education (§1), the young Basini falls into dehumanization (§ 2) under the blows of a barbaric mob (§ 3).

II – The Confusions of Young Törless sense fascism

§ 1 – Abstract of Robert Musil's novel

Revolving around the issue of education, this dark and disrupted chronicle recounts the life of a lost young man wondering about social morality and its meaning. *The Confusions of Young Törless* foreshadows totalitarianism. The characters Reiting and Beineberg are young, sadistic and pervert barbaric who represent a perfect example of inhuman in Man. Apparently moderate and kind during the day, these pupils proceed unscrupulously at night and assault the student Basini.

Törless, with Reiting and Beineberg, acts as a passive witness. Although Törless seeks the meaning of human condition he is without any morality. In spite of his quest for comprehension no answer satisfies him.

§ 2 – Archetype of a dehumanization

Robert Musil is concerned with the relationships between the pupils of the military college W. This small social entity is based on the competition spirit.

There, the pupils' behavior is ranked between conformed and marginal at the risk of exclusion.
Törless adapts very well to the point of holding a preponderant position in the alliance of the two strong pupils, Reiting and Beineberg.

A secret attic provides the space for the sadistic power of the trio. In this diabolical space, the student Basini features the masochistic scapegoat suffering the worse abuses on the grounds of punishment for a theft of money. Törless lives through the experience as an observer although he feels split by various feelings (helplessness, compassion, indifference and contempt).

Visibly lacking in the two torturers, ambivalence is present in Törless withheld by his superego: "(He) *had not moved from his position. At the very beginning, yet, a bestial desire surged in him to jump and strike with the others, but the feeling he would arrive too late, that he would be superfluous restrained him. As if a heavy grasp had paralyzed him*" (69).

An object of multiple experiments by Reiting and Beineberg, Basini turns into a sexual slave and progressively dehumanizes himself. This student embodies the archetype of the martyr whose ambivalent behavior questions the position of victim… In any case, his dehumanization prefigures the collective barbarity committed by the Nazis.

§ 3 – The mob of three "without-other"
   at the beginning of the 20th century

The specific behavior of each of the three characters towards Basini expresses their relation to the world. They already are "neo-subjects" who objectify others...
Reiting is friendly as well as "*tyrannic, merciless to anyone resisting him*" (69). In a nutshell, Reiting uses Basini as an antidot to his impulses. Supposedly to "*learn about the soul*", Beineberg manipulates Basini through hypnosis.

The common point of their opposite and complementary behavior resides in their certitude.
In front of these two individuals – gifted, resolute, mature but immoderate – Törless seeks to situate himself. His outburst against Basini is more delicate but more hypocritical.

First, as if he was more 'socialized', he questions Basini's feeling facing so many degradations demeaning his personality.

After he has experienced his homosexual attraction for Basini in secret, Törless assumes a new behavior and discovers shame…

Less confident than Reiting and Beineberg, the "hero" shows up more subtle and… contradictory. Like a synthesis of the other two, his link is dual. The student Törless goes in opposite directions because he wants to understand the Other and the World.

From questions to impulses, Törless tries to understand himself between the "father-mode" and the "mother-mode". And so, he does falter between *the Thing* and the word: sometimes he obeys to the bodily; sometimes he obeys to reason, he intellectualizes... However, his try towards the "father-mode" fails. The student gets lost in the confusion of the language as, in the same time, reality, turning foggy and mysterious, escapes him. His continuous hesitation between sense-reason and its fogginess certifies his problem to bear the unutterable part of speech.

Törless searches for the solution of the contradiction between sensuality and intellect. But he is lost in an inextricable duality between *the Thing* that seems real when perceived and the word about the Thing that chases him away... from *the Thing*.

By the carnal bond Törless gives himself the illusion of entering Basini's intellect. However, he gives in to the bodily impulse without offering any love. He denies his love to Basini. Törless fails to unite opposites in himself because he objectifies the other. And the magnetism of Basini over him dissolves... Moreover this "without-other" of 1906 leaves the school without any shame or remorse. As a matter of fact, to succeed in reuniting and leaving the mob the adolescent Törless still lacks a way to a third term: Morality.

Confused and tormented, Törless is in an internal war (*).

He is seeking to light the torch of his conscience in this attic where the cruel Reiting and Beineberg torture Basini: "***The lantern** being overturned, its light spread out on the floor at Törless' feet, lazily indifferent*" (69).

Unfortunately, Törless' **lantern** is tumbled as his morality...

(*) "**War**" *comes from the Germanic word "werra", "guerra" in Spanish and in Italian; and "wirre" means "confusion" in German, "wirren" means "to scramble". "Bellum" in its archaic Latin form "duellum" comes from the Indo-European root "dau", "to torment", "to burn"; also from "daio", "I light" and from "daidos", "the torch".*

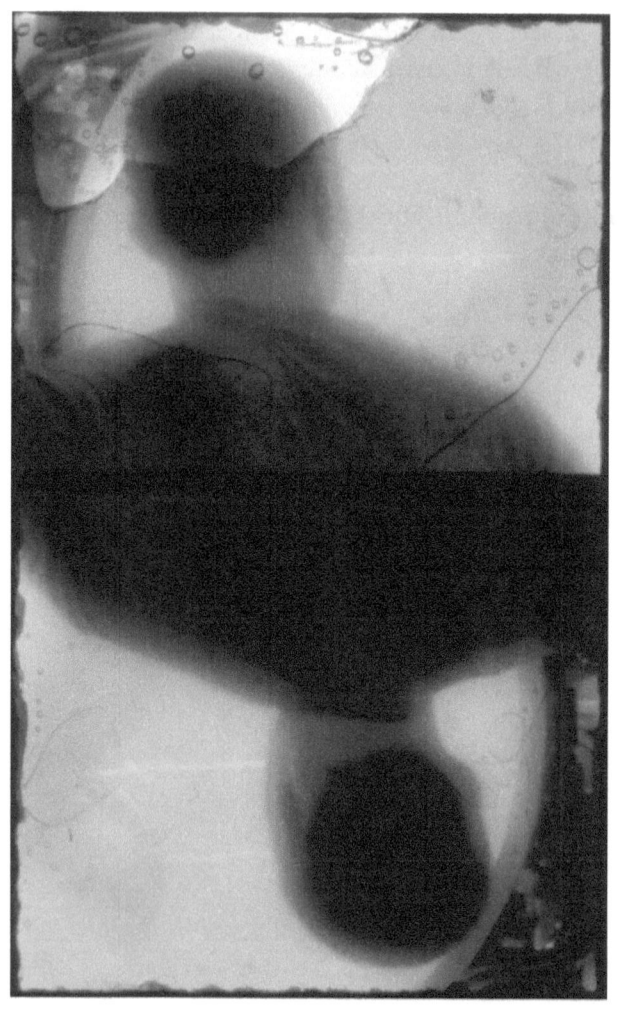

The lantern is a symbol of Knowledge enlightening Man and protecting the frail fire of Spirit. This lantern comes to life again in *Guernica* (70) in the triple form of a ceiling light, a lamp and a torch. An electric ceiling light as an allegory of the death drive; an oil lamp as a metaphor of libido. And as a synthesis of hope a torch held by a woman divine messenger, incarnating a future of brightness and… Freedom.

Not far from the woman, in the center of the masterpiece, a horse violently neighs the People's pain.

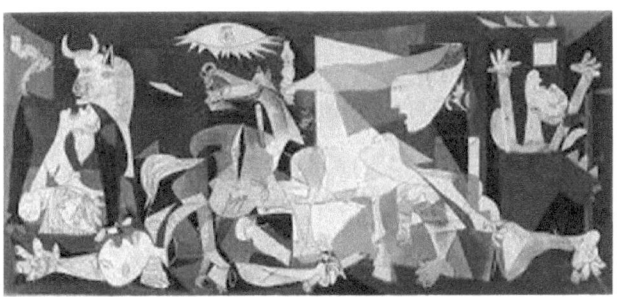

(70) PICASSO Pablo – *Guernica*

Picasso uses his brush as others take arms (§ 1) to paint the inhuman (§ 2) and the Human gathered by an historical Beauty (§ 3).

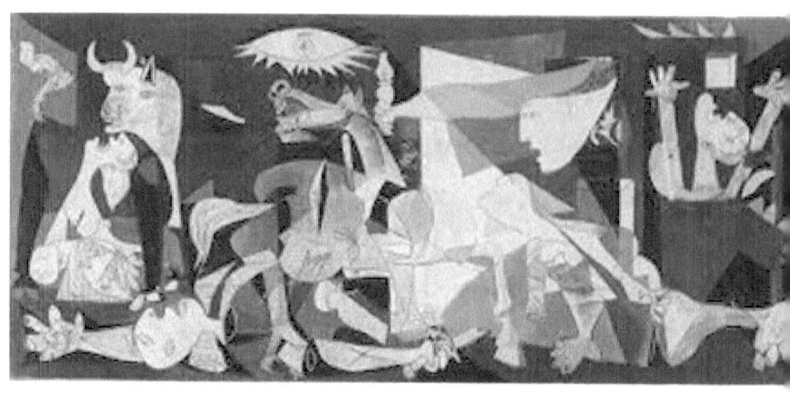

(70) PICASSO Pablo – *Guernica* (1937), huile (349,3 x 776 cm) – Madrid, Museo Nacional Centro de Arte Reina Sofia

III – *Guernica:* painting History and the inhuman in Man

§ 1 – Drawing and color: weapons against the war

The 20th century and the two world wars interrogate Picasso's political engagement. With *Guernica*, his artistic approach initiates a new reflection about History painting. Already his blue period testifies by his models of poor people and other outsiders of his social conscience. The topic of war is numerous in his work aiming mainly to show the grim sacrifice of peoples.

The Mass Grave (71) – about extermination camps – does not even single out the bodies of mothers, children or fathers, inhumanly murdered…

He paints inhumanity of war in *Massacre in Korea* (72) clearly related to Goya 's *Tres de Mayo* (73). In an allusive manner, *The Crying Woman* (74) – as an echo of the Spanish Civil War – also symbolizes human pain and despair.

His disillusion often leads him to a return to Painting only: *Guernica* gives an answer by art to History's traumas. Picasso turns into an allegory the revolt against dictature: "*I am proud to say it, I never considered Painting as an art of simple pleasure, of entertainment; I wanted by drawing and color, since those were my weapons, to penetrate always more ahead in the knowledge of the world and of men, so that this knowledge liberates us more every day (…). Yes, I have conscience to have always fought by my painting as a genuine revolutionary*" (75).

Guernica is one the rare commands accepted by Picasso. In 1937, the Spanish government asks him a work for the opening of the Spanish building in the International fair of the arts and technics in modern life. The art critic Christian Zervos supports Guernica with an enlightened text in his Cahiers d'art (76): however, the work remains confidential. The fresco goes on a tour of exhibits but, mainly, as a property of Spain, it is used to collect money for the republican army.

Together with war's outbreak in Europe, the legitimation of *Guernica* occurs from its touring in the United States in 1939. This series of exhibits leads to the retrospective *Pablo Picasso: forty years of his Art* at the *Museum of Modern Art* of New York (November 1939-January 1940).

The critics value Guernica as one of the art masterpieces of the 20th century. Picasso lends the work to the MOMA on the condition to give it back to Spain when the Republic will be restored. Only in 1981, eight years after the artist's death, *Guernica* returns to its country to be temporarily exposed in Madrid in an annex of the Prado, the *Cason del Buen retiro*. Guernica and its preparatory works settle, at last, in 1992, at the *Museo Nacional Centro de Arte Reina Sofia*.

§ 2 – Premonition of barbary

For his choice of the subject of *Guernica*, Picasso takes a long time and finds inspiration in the communist daily newspaper, *Ce Soir*. An illustrated article shows the shelling, by the German planes under the Caudillo's orders, of the Basque village of *Guernica* on April 28th 1937.

This news turns quickly, for the Spanish population, into a banner of its fight for freedom. For Europe the event becomes a prophetic allegory of the blackness to come.

On the first drawing of May 1st 1937, the artist sets the major protagonists of his fresco; the woman at the window holding a torch, the horse and the bull. At once, Picasso affirms his desire to create a universal symbol of human pain. In eleven days, near fifteen preparatory drawings draw a precise scheme in a surface always more compressed. On May 8th, the mother with a dead child appears. On the 11th, the artist transfers the drawing n° 15 on the canvas and starts to paint. Then, Picasso achieves painting *Guernica* in 24 days.

The horizontal format of the fresco displays a horizon of History built of black, white and grey. In a long panoramic of nearly 8 meters, the pyramidal composition considers Painting as the space of Man's evolution between life and death. This pyramid orders the work by the figure of a major antagonism between an interior duality and a tremendous balance. Antonio Oriol Anguerra (77) identifies an organization of the nine figures of Guernica in three specific sections: the "*three meaningless deaths*" (a woman, a child, a man), the "*three desperate screams*" (the mother with child, the bird and the horse) and the "*three obsolete symbols*" (Religion, Power and Wisdom).

The content of the work, although much imposing, seems to be constrained like Man is socialized by Culture.

The painting's stability is set by horizontal-vertical-oblique lines and directions, up, down and depth.

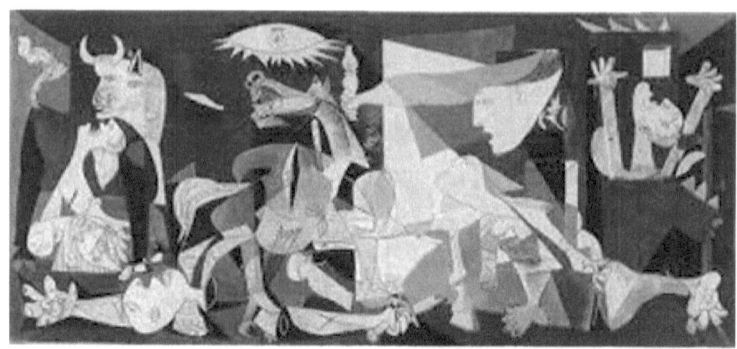

A horizontal line of hands, arms, feet and legs forms the stable base of the pyramid. Central and on the ground across is drawn on a severed arm holding a broken sword... Sign that the death drive is at its highest level.

Vertical lines are numerous. For example, on the left, a corpse's open hand seems to support the head of a dead child carried by his mother while a vertical line continues from the screaming mother up to the bull.

Equally diverse oblique lines energize the ensemble. Like the one that recovers the vital momentum in the delineation of a dead's head on the ground towards a horse's head topped by the light of a lamp. Dual movements associate to create a secret tension (two diagonals, two crying women).

The whole surface appears resolute and coerced all at once. Guernica's monumental composition unrolls a strip of trilogies. Following a rhythm 3-2-1, Picasso articulates the hope inspired by a conjunction of opposites.

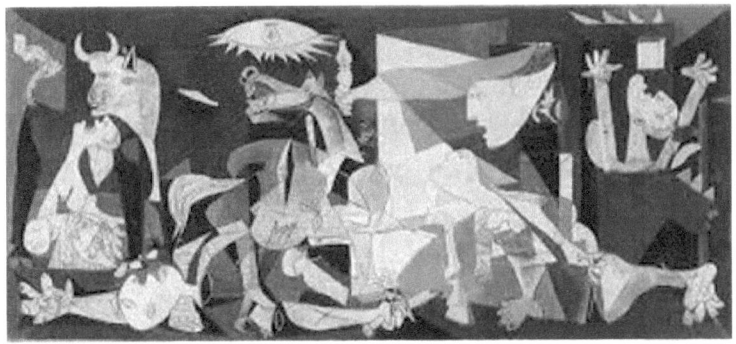

The first formal trilogy emerges from an asserted horizontal line, quite terrestrial and of Mother-mode, that spreads from the imploring figure with the arm holding the lamp to the dead child and the warrior.

Three vertical lines, celestial and of Father-mode, confront each other and fragment the expanse: on the right and on the left two women scream and… a bull – avid untamed male – erects.

This horizontal and vertical framework invigorates *Guernica* by apparent and hidden motions.
The synthesis appears in a pyramid thanks to two strong diagonals leading to the lamp.

As a matter of fact the oblique on the left goes up from the warrior' hand – engraved with a devilishly inverted star – to the dead child's face, follows the edge of a dark table and reaches the light.

On the right the other oblique follows the path traced by the hand, the arm and the neck of the imploring figure up to the lantern.

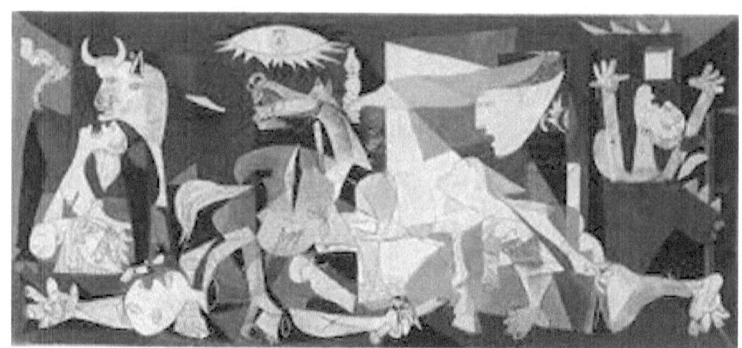

Simultaneously stable and tense, the pyramid conveys to the whole canvas a dual tension between high and low and channels the ensemble of variations. This second trilogy builds up on a structure background which leaves a feeling of abyss, of confusion… and of union, of accord between inside and outside, between front and back.

The fresco gives the feeling of a permanent oscillation united and divided, vast and oppressed. However, *Guernica* remains thwarted… as a figure of destruction.

The spectator is facing his own internal duality and the chaos of an external war. To save himself of this ambivalence, his function is to decipher the multiple ways opened in a labyrinth of signs: bodies, animals, screams, electric light and oil lamp's light, etc.

§ 3 – A History Painting

Freeing himself of anecdote – notwithstanding the title – and by the monumentality of Guernica, Picasso competes with History painting especially the specific genre of Battle painting.

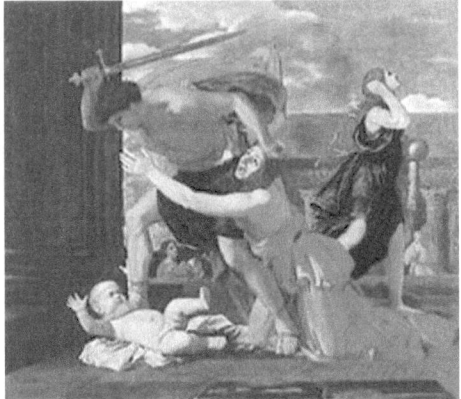

(79) POUSSIN Nicolas – *Le massacre des innocents* (entre 1625 et 1632), huile sur toile (147 x 171 cm) – Musée Condé

"Inside this overall scheme, references to art history are nearly infinite" according to the critic Guitemie Maldonado (78). As a matter of fact, there is a suite of homages: from Poussin's *Massacre of the Innocents* (79) to Goya's *Disasters of War* (54) and *El Trrès de Mayo* (73) evoked by the arms' gestures.

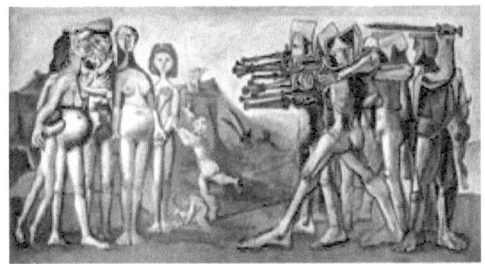

(72) PICASSO Pablo – *Massacre en Corée* (1951), huile sur contreplaqué (109,5 x 209,5 cm) – Paris, Musée Picasso

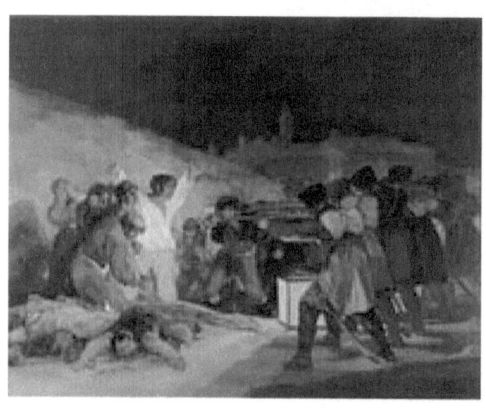

(73) GOYA Francisco de – *Tres de Mayo* ou *Le 3 mai 1808* (1814), huile (2,66 x 3,45 m) – Musée du Prado de Madrid

20th century's collective conscience wags in the chaos of Spanish War. The moral sense accuses the disproportion of the powers and the contribution borne by the Spanish people. Picasso paints a tree of sorrows that makes History in Painting.

Guernica forme un condensé pictural du tragique humain imaginé sous de multiples doubles sens : individuel-collectif, conjoncturel-symbolique, tradition-modernité, humain-inhumain... "*En un rectangle noir et blanc telle que nous apparaît l'antique tragédie, Picasso nous envoie notre lettre de deuil : tout ce que nous aimons va mourir, et c'est pourquoi il était à ce point nécessaire que tout ce que nous aimons se résumât, comme l'effusion des grands adieux, en quelque chose d'inoubliablement beau*" (80).

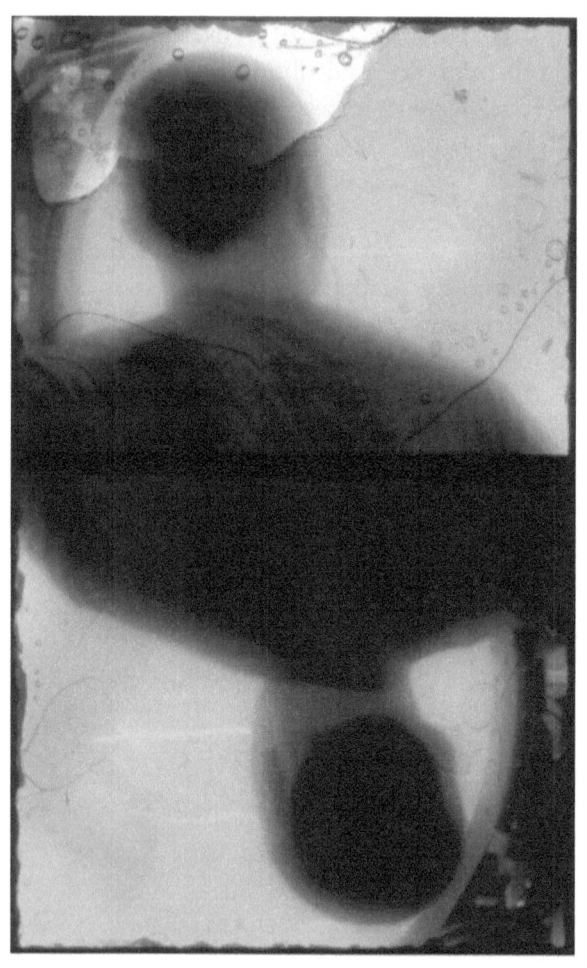

Man experiences an everlasting internal war of desire whose Culture bears the bitter fruits with death drive.

This human ambivalence however reveals a dynamics that the double foundation of language mobilizes. The Mother-Father modes activate the power of being on the condition to accept a moderate prevalence of the Father language.

Inversely, the excess of the Mother language unsettles the 21st century. Narcissus' omnipotence hurts Civilization under the yoke of an inhuman financial capitalism.

Barbarism is actually inscribed in Human. Today, and forever, the Human – 'primitive' or 'civilized' – bears in oneself the inhuman. Man's inhumanity is a constitutive part of the being that operates the Individual as well as the Society.
But, internal as well as external, war is always the full use of the death drive.

This inhuman nested in the Human underlines its most imperious dualism situated between the social constraint and the personal enjoyment. History and current events permanently prove this reality. At all event, Culture – yes, imperfect and frail – implements a solution.

"It is in the chaos of war that the harmony of union and solidarity rises. It is in front of death's violence, the immemorial Thanatos, that the power of desire, the immemorial Eros, soars" (81).

Art masterworks that unveil the tragedy of human condition provide a synthesis of the opposites between *the Thing* and the paternal metaphor.

The Thing does constitute one of the conditions useful to social constructions – religious, juridical, artistic or political – but its scattered chaos requires to hold it back like an animal. The control of *The Thing* intersects with the Law of the Father and its necessary return in the contemporary society.

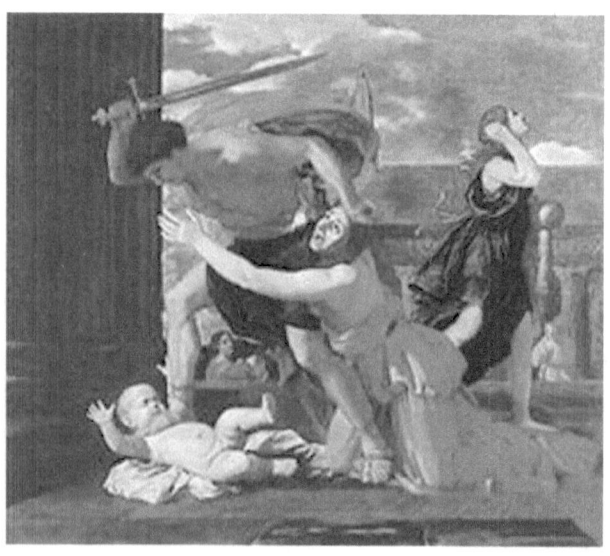

(79) POUSSIN, *Le massacre des innocents*

In front of this elusive magma, the spirit must regain the control over the matter. *"What the Mouth of Darkness says"* (82) may be too influential over the spiritual in Man.

*"As well as in the marshes asleep under the woods
In more than one soul, one may see two things together
The sky, that dyes the barely stirred waters
With its rays and all its clouds
And the mud, bleak, awful, dark and dormant bottom
Where black reptiles vaguely swarm"*

(68) GOYA, *Le chien dans le gouffre*

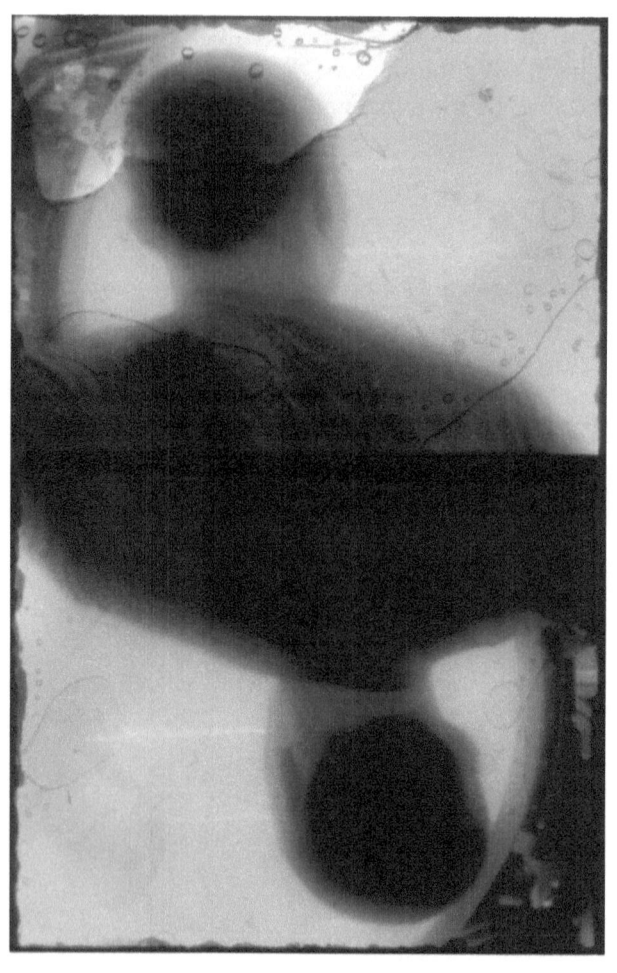

Bernard Gast - *La bascule*

Bibliographical references & Illustrations

Introduction

(1) NIETZSCHE Friedrich – *Ecce Homo* (1888), traduit par H. Albert et A.-M. Desrousseaux – http://fr.wikisource.org/wiki/Humain,_trop_humain (page 483)
(2) FREUD Sigmund – *Actuelles sur la guerre et la mort*, 1915 – in *Essais de psychanalyse* (S. Jankelevitch), *Chapitre I* (p. 219 à 235) = p. 227 – Payot, 1951
(2 bis) FREUD Sigmund – *Pulsions et destins des pulsions* (1915) – Gallimard, collection Folio Essais, p. 11 à 43

Part 1 – The individual's affective ambivalence: perpetual intimate conflict of desire

I – About the human

(3) LACAN Jacques – *Note italienne*, in *Autres écrits* (1973) – Seuil p. 311
(4) LACAN Jacques – *Fonction et champ de la parole et du langage en psychanalyse*, 1953, in *La psychanalyse*, volume I, 1956, PUF p. 81-166 et in *Écrits*, SEUIL, 1966, p 155
(5) LACAN Jacques – *Le triomphe de la religion*, Paris, Seuil, 2005 et *la troisième*, *Lettres de l'EFP*, n° 18, 1975
(5 bis) In 1971, Jacques Lacan contracts "the language" into "**thelanguage**" and by this neologism names **the language of the unconscious** - Lire aussi "*La naissance de lalangue*" sur *https://www.cairn.info/revue-essaim-2012-2-page-7.htm*
(6) LACAN Jacques – *L'objet de la psychanalyse*, Livre XIII (1965-1966) – Seuil
(7) LACAN Jacques – *Le séminaire, livre IV : La relation d'objet* (1956-1957) – Seuil
(8) LACAN Jacques – *Encore, Le Séminaire*, Livre XX (1972-1973) – Seuil, p 114
(9) KANT Emmanuel (1724-1804) – *Fondements de la métaphysique des moeurs* (1785), traduit par Victor Delbos – Librairie Vrin, in Première section : *Passage de la connaissance rationnelle commune de la moralité à la connaissance philosophique* : p. 55 à 73

II – About the inhuman

(10) MONTAIGNE Michel de (1533-1592) – *Les essais* (1572-1592), in *Chapitre XXXI : Des cannibales* et in *Livre III, chapitre VI : Des coches* – Traduction en français moderne par A. Lanly – Gallimard, Collection Quarto
(11) PLAUTE Titus Maccius (254-184 avant J.C.) – *Asinaria* ou *La Comédie des ânes* (env. 195 avant J.C.) – Trad. Alfred Ernout – Les belles lettres
(12) ERASMUS DESIDERIUS Roterodamus, dit ERASME (1466?-1536) – *Les Adages* – Les Belles Lettres
(13) RABELAIS François (1483?-1553) – *Le Tiers Livre des faits et dits Héroïques du noble Pantagruel : composés par M. François Rabelais, Docteur en Médecine, et Calloier des Iles d'Hyeres* (1546) – Edition numérisée : http://www.bvh.univ-tours.fr/Consult/index.asp?numfiche=61&numtable=BMT_3537

(14) AGRIPPA D'AUBIGNE Théodore (1552-1630) – *Les Tragiques* (1616) – Gallimard, coll. "Poésie", in Livre I
(15) BACON FRANCIS (1561-1626) – *Novum Organum* (1620), notes de MM Malherbe et Pousseur – PUF Epiméthée
(16) HOBBES Thomas (1588-1679) – *De cive (Le Citoyen)*, ou les fondements de la politique (1642) in Préface – Edition électronique sur http://classiques.uqac.ca/classiques/hobbes_thomas/le_citoyen/citoyen_preface.html – "*Je montre d'abord que l'état des hommes sans société civile (quel état peut être nommé l'état naturel) est rien sauf une guerre de tous contre tous*"
(17) SCHOPENHAUER – *Le Monde comme Volonté et comme Représentation* (1819) http://fr.wikisource.org/wiki/Le_Monde_comme_volonté_et_comme_représentation
(18) FREUD Sigmund – *Malaise dans la culture (Le)*, (1930), PUF
(19) ROUSSEAU Jean-Jacques – *Discours sur l'origine et les fondements de l'inégalité parmi les hommes* (1755), présenté par Jacques Roger – GF Flammarion
(20) ROUSSEAU Jean-Jacques (1712-1778) – *Émile, ou De l'éducation* (1762) par Michel LAUNAY – Garnier-Flammarion
(21) SENEQUE – *Lettres à Lucilius*, XCV, 33
(22) FREUD Sigmund – *Une difficulté de la psychanalyse* (1917) in *Essais de psychanalyse* – Payot
(24) FREUD Sigmund – *Au-delà du principe de plaisir* (1920), *Essais de psychanalyse*, Payot (Jankélévitch), p. 5
(25) FREUD Sigmund – *Psychanalyse et théorie de la libido*, (1923), *Résultats, idées, problèmes* – Tome II PUF

III – The law of opposites and ambivalence: positive impact of negative

(26) FREUD Sigmund – *Le moi et le ça* (1923), *Essais de psychanalyse*, Payot (Jankélévitch) *Moi et le Soi* p 163
(27) FREUD Sigmund – *Le problème économique du masochisme* (1924) *Névrose, psychose et perversion* – PUF
(28) FREUD Sigmund, EINSTEIN Albert – *Pourquoi la guerre ?* (1932) in *Résultats, idées, problèmes,* T. II – PUF, p. 203-216 (Lettre ouverte sous l'impulsion de l'*Institut international de coopération intellectuelle* en lien avec la *S.D.N.*, dans le dessein de fortifier l'action pour la paix)
(28 bis) FREUD Sigmund – *Psychologie des masses et analyse du moi* (1921), in *Essais de psychanalyse*, Payot (Jankélévitch), p. 76-162, (Freud rappelle dans *Pourquoi la guerre ?* les identifications évoquées dans cet écrit)
(29) FREUD Sigmund – *Nouvelle suite des conférences d'introduction à la psychanalyse* (1933), Gallimard
(30) FREUD Sigmund – *L'analyse finie et l'analyse sans fin* (1937), *Résultats, idées, problèmes* – PUF, t. II
(31) FREUD Sigmund – *Abrégé de psychanalyse* (1938) – PUF
(31 bis) ASSOUN P-L – *Dictionnaire des œuvres psychanalytiques* – PUF, p 956 à 961
(32) FREUD Sigmund – *Introduction à "Sur la psychanalyse des névroses de guerre"* (1919) (*Einleitung zu "Zur Psychoanalyse der Kriegsneurosen"*), in *Résultats, idées, problèmes*, I, PUF pages 243–247

(33) FREUD Sigmund – *Totem et Tabou, quelques concordances entre la vie psychique des sauvages et des névrosés* (1913) – Payot p 18
(33 bis) LEVI-STRAUSS Claude, *Les structures élémentaires de la parenté* 1949), *in 2 (problème de l'inceste)* – PUF
(34) ENRIQUEZ Eugène, *DE LA HORDE A L'ETAT, Essai de psychanalyse du lien social* – Nrf/Gallimard, p 38
(35) LEGENDRE Pierre – *Jouir du pouvoir. Traité de bureaucratie patriote* (1976) – Coll. *Critique*, éditions de Minuit
(35 bis) HERACLITE (vers 544-480 av. J.C.) – *Fragments* (traduction et notes Jean-François Pradeau) – Flammarion GF
(36) FREUD Sigmund – *Dostoïevski et le parricide* (1928) – in *Résultats, idées, problèmes*, tome II, p. 161-180 – PUF
(37) FREUD – *L'homme Moïse et la religion monothéiste* – Gallimard pages 21, 213
(37 bis) HEIDEGGER Martin – *Essais et conférences* (1949), traduit de l'Allemand par André Préau et préfacé par Jean Beaufret – nrf Gallimard. L'original est paru à Pfulligen en 1954 sous le titre : *Vortrage und Aufsatze*. Les quatre conférences de Martin Heidegger ont eu lieu au Club de Brême (décembre 1949) sous l'appellation générale *Einblick in das was ist* (*Regard dans ce qui est*). Parution dans le tome 79 de la *Gesamtausgabe, Bremer und Freiburger Vorträge*. Les conférences se présentaient dans l'ordre suivant : *das Ding* (La chose), *das Gestell* (Le dispositif), *die Gefhar* (Le péril) et *Die Kehre* (Le tournant) – En ligne sur : https://prepasaintsernin.files.wordpress.com/2020/06/heidegger-essais-et-confc3a9rences.pdf
(37 ter) HEIDEGGER – *Chemins qui ne mènent nulle part* (1950) – Gallimard p. 79
(38) LACAN Jacques – *L'éthique de la psychanalyse, Le Séminaire VII* (1959-1960) – Seuil pages 85, 101, 201 à 227
(39) CHEMAMA Roland – VANDERMERSCH Bernard – *La Chose* in *Dictionnaire de la Psychanalyse* – Larousse
(40) FREUD Sigmund – *Actuelles sur la guerre et la mort* (1915) in *Essais de psychanalyse* (S. Jankelevitch), in *IV, Chapitre II - Notre attitude à l'égard de la mort* – Payot, 1951, p. 238 et p. 250

Part 2 – Contemporary impact of human ambivalence: a society without father

I – The tyranny of abusive narcissism

(41) LEBRUN J-P – *La perversion ordinaire. Vivre ensemble sans autrui*, Denoël 2007
(42) MELMAN Charles – *L'homme sans gravité*, entretien avec J-P Lebrun, Denoël
(43) MELMAN Charles – *La nouvelle économie psychique* avec J-Pierre Lebrun, Erès
(44) DELEUZE – *Michel Tournier et le monde sans-autrui* – Logique du sens, Minuit
(45) TOURNIER Michel – *Vendredi ou les limbes du Pacifique* (1967) – Folio
(46) FREUD Sigmund – Préface au livre de AICHHORN August – *Jeunes en souffrance* (1925) Champ social p. 6
(47) FORGET J-M – *L'adolescent face à ses actes Et aux autres* – Erès 2005 p. 116
(48) LACAN – *Congrès sur les psychoses de l'enfant* (1968) – Denoël, *L'espace analytique*
(49) SZLAMOWICZ Jean – *Les moutons de la pensée* – Cerf 2022

II – The fragmented Man and the consequences

(50) DE GAULEJAC Vincent – LENOETTI Taboada – *La lutte des places* (1994) – Desclée de Brouwer
(51) RABHI Pierre – *Vers la sobriété heureuse* (2010) – Actes sud

Part 3 – Art as a sublimated synthesis of human ambivalence

(52) PRAZ Mario (1896-1982) – *La Chair, la Mort et le Diable dans la littérature romantique* (1930) – Gallimard/Tel
(52 bis) DECONCHAT André – *Goya, graveur des lumières* (2008) – Dossier de l'art n° 151, avril 2008, p. 59-69
(52 ter) TODOROV Tzvetan – *Goya à l'ombre des lumières* – Flammarion

I – Goya, the "disenchanter": the dark background of Human

(53) GOYA Francisco de – *Les Caprices* (1799) – 80 gravures : eau-forte et aquatinte, Francfort-sur-le-Main, Städel Museum
(54) GOYA – *Les désastres de la guerre* (1810-1820) – 1re éd., 1863, eau-forte, pointe sèche, burin et brunissoir, Francfort-sur-le-Main, Städel Museum
(55) GOYA, un regard libre – *Catalogue des expositions* de Lille au Palais des Beaux-Arts (12 décembre 1998-14 mars 1999) et de Philadelphie au Philadelphia Museum of Art (17 avril 1999-11 juillet 1999) avec le commissariat d'Arnauld Brejon de Lavergnée et Joseph J. Rishel – RMN (Réunion des Musées Nationaux) – Article d'Yves Bonnefoy : *Goya pour la fin du siècle* p. 42
(56) CUESTA M. Cano – *Goya en la Fundacion Lazaro Galdiano* (1999), Madrid
(57) GOYA Francisco de – *Capricho* n° 23 : *Aquellos polvos* in *Les Caprices* (1799) L'inquisition se sent attaquée pour la mention : *Aquellos polvos (Ces poussières)... Trajeron estos lodos (transportèrent ces boues)*. Obscure allusion du titre, en un double sens orienté contre le parquet, et non contre l'inculpé.
(58) GOYA Francisco de – *Capricho* n° 1 : *Francisco Goya y Lucientes, Pintor* in *Les Caprices* (1799) – Francfort-sur-le-Main, Städel Museum
(59) GOYA – *Capricho* n° 6 : *Nadie se conoce* in *Les Caprices* (1799) – Déjà cité
(60) GOYA Francisco de – *Capricho* n° 43 : *El sueño de la razón produce monstruos* in *Les Caprices* (1799) – Déjà cité ci-dessus – "*...El Autor soñando. Su intento solo es desterrar vulgaridades perjudiciales y perpetuar con esta obra de caprichos, el testimonio sólido de la verdad*" – This *Capricho* was almost the cover of the 80 *Caprichos*.
(61) GOYA – *Capricho* n° 13 : *Estan calientes* in *Les Caprices* (1799) – Déjà cité
(62) GOYA Francisco de – *Capricho* n° 42 : *Tu que no puedes* (*Toi qui ne peux pas*) in *Les Caprices* (1799) – Country people supporting happy donkeys, evoke the politics of classes divided between the inactive (religious, nobles) and the people.
(63) GOYA Francisco de – *Capricho* n° 63 : *Miren que graves !* (*Regardez comme c'est sérieux !*) in *Les Caprices* (1799) – (the country-dwellers are donkeys ridden by monsters including a bird of prey. Agrarian reform in failure, these slaves discover themselves exploited by aristocratic, and religious voracity).
(64) GOYA – *Capricho* n° 37 à 42 : *Asnerias* in *Les Caprices* (1799) – Déjà cité

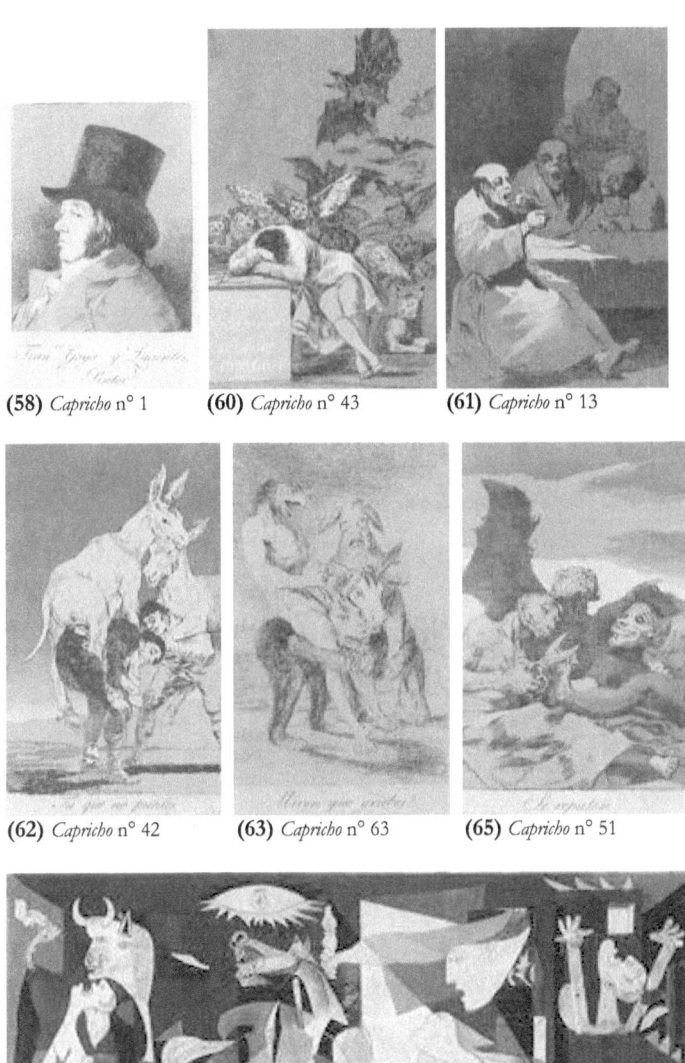

(58) *Capricho* n° 1   (60) *Capricho* n° 43   (61) *Capricho* n° 13

(62) *Capricho* n° 42   (63) *Capricho* n° 63   (65) *Capricho* n° 51

(70) PICASSO Pablo – *Guernica* (1937), huile (349,3 x 776 cm)

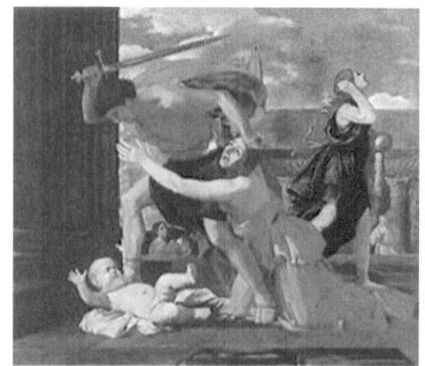

(79) POUSSIN, *Le massacre des innocents* (68) GOYA, *Le chien dans le gouffre*

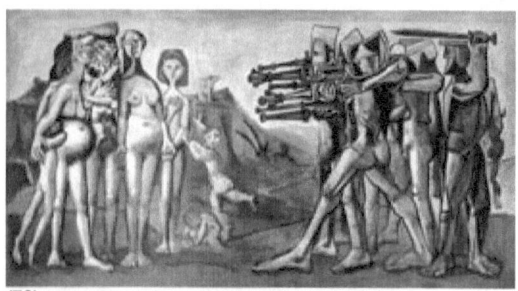

(72) PICASSO Pablo – *Massacre en Corée* (1951)

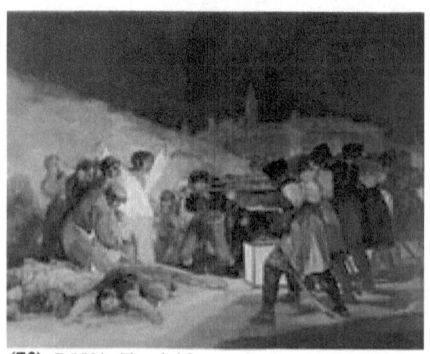

(73) GOYA, *Tres de Mayo* ou *Le 3 mai 1808* (1814)

(65) GOYA Francisco de – *Capricho* n° 51 : *Se repulen* in *Les Caprices* (1799) – Déjà cité – A monster cuts someone else's nails while a third one deploys his elders... Either the reminder of the forbidden by witchcraft to have long fingernails (*Prado Manuscript*), or an acerbic critique of the state (*Ayala Manuscript*), or a caricature of fraudulent employees (*Manuscrit de la Bibliothèque Nationale d'Espagne*).
(66) SCHNEEDE Uwe M. – *Internationale du Surréalisme*, Paris (1938), In Bernd Klüser, Katharina Hegewisch: Die Kunst der Ausstellung. Eine Dokumentation dreißig exemplarischer Kunstausstellungen dieses Jahrhunderts
(67) MALRAUX André – *Les Voix du silence* (1936-1951) – nrf/Gal. de la Pléiade
(68) GOYA – *Le chien dans le gouffre* (*Peintures noires* : 1819-1823) – Prado, Madrid

II – The Confusions of Young Törless sense fascism

(69) MUSIL Robert (1880-1942) – *Les désarrois de l'élève Törless* (1906) – Points Seuil p. 61 et 113

III – *Guernica***: painting History and inhuman in Man**

(70) PICASSO Pablo – *Guernica* (1937), huile (349,3 x 776 cm) – Madrid, Museo Nacional Centro de Arte Reina Sofia
(71) PICASSO Pablo – *Le charnier* (1944), huile et fusain (199,8 x 250,1 cm) – New York, The Museum of Modern Art
(72) PICASSO Pablo – *Massacre en Corée* (1951), huile sur contreplaqué (109,5 x 209,5 cm) – Paris, Musée Picasso
(73) GOYA Francisco de – *Tres de Mayo* ou *Le 3 mai 1808* (1814), huile (2,66 x 3,45 m) – Musée du Prado de Madrid
(74) PICASSO Pablo – *La femme qui pleure* (26 octobre 1937), huile sur toile (59,5 x 49 cm) – Londres, Tate Modern
(75) PICASSO – *Why I became a Communist* (1944), *New Masses*, 24-10-1944, p. 11
(76) ZERVOS Christian (1889-1970) – *Guernica* (1937) – Cahiers d'art, 4-5
(77) ORIOL ANGUERA Antonio – *Guernica* (1979), Société Française du Livre
(78) MALDONADO Guitemie – *Lire la peinture de Picasso* (2007) – Larousse
(79) POUSSIN Nicolas – *Le massacre des innocents* (entre 1625 et 1632), huile sur toile (147 x 171 cm) – Musée Condé
(80) LEIRIS Michel – *Faire-part* (1937), dans le *Cahiers d'art* sur *Guernica & Un génie sans piédestal et autres écrits sur Picasso*, présentés par M.-L Bernadac – Fourbis

Conclusion

(81) LOISON Raphaël, poète, traducteur & écrivain, fidèle ami de longue date
(82) HUGO Victor (1802-1885) – *Œuvres poétiques, Les Contemplations,* Livre VI, poème XXVI – *Ce que dit la Bouche d'Ombre* (1855) – Edition et présentation de Pierre Albouy – *La pléiade 1967*

About the author

Bernard Gast is an artist, philosopher and psychoanalyst

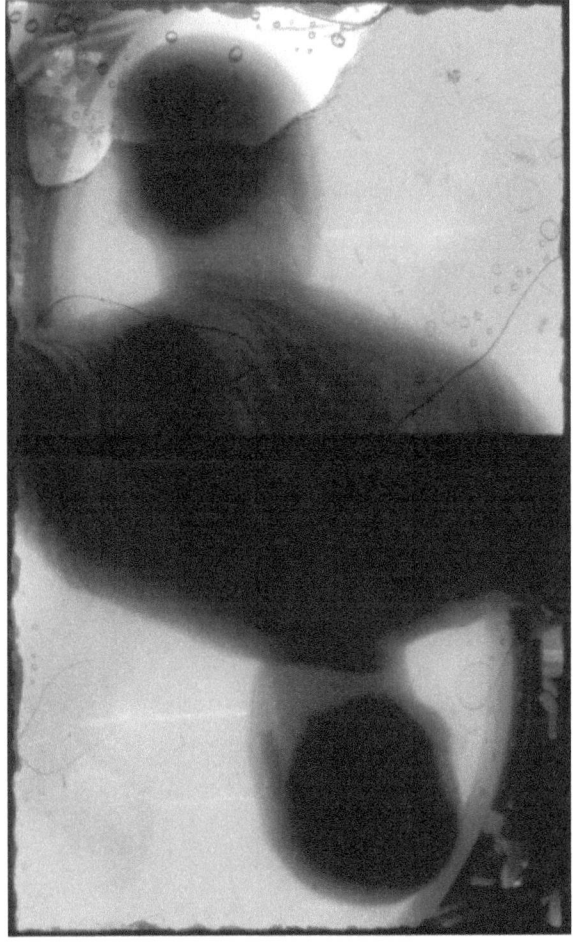

La bascule (2011) - *Painting-with-Cinema* (1 x 1,30 m) © Bernard Gast

The inhuman or war within Man

Copyright © I Gallery Editions

All rights reserved
ISBN : 9798356170904

The inhuman or war within Man
Bernard Gast

Essays (Philosophy & Aesthetics)
© I Gallery Editions 2022

igalleryeditions@free.fr

In
I GALLERY EDITIONS
by
Collection

Novel
Fumi BIGOT – *La maison des beaux dormants*

Well-being & Cooking
Bessie COOK – *Mini-recettes pour maigrir*

Essays
Anonyme médiéval – *Le Royaume* (Spirituality)
Bernard GAST – *L'inhumain ou la guerre en l'Homme* (Philosophy)
Bernard GAST – *The inhuman or war within Man* (Philosophy)
Marc VAUTHIER – *L'industrie de demain et la dépollution des sols* (Science)

Art
Anne MICHALSON – *La Peinture avec le Cinéma de Bernard Gast*

Contact : igalleryeditions@free.fr

www.ingramcontent.com/pod-product-compliance
Lightning Source LLC
Chambersburg PA
CBHW020449220526
45464CB00002B/921